Fruit for Eternity

Fruit for Eternity

Ashley Schmierer

New Wine Press

New Wine Ministries
PO Box 17
Chichester
West Sussex
United Kingdom
PO19 2AW

Scripture quotations are taken from the following version of the Bible:
New King James Bible. Copyright © 1979, 1980, 1982
by Thomas Nelson, Inc. Used by permission. All rights reserved.

ISBN 978-1-905991-53-2

Typeset by **documen**, www.documen.co.uk
Cover design by CCD, www.ccdgroup.co.uk
Printed in the United Kingdom

About the Author

As a fruit grower, Ashley Schmierer heard God speak, "If you follow Me, you will have fruit for eternity." He and his wife, Ruth, left their farming business to be trained for ministry and later pastored a church in Innisfail, Australia. During this time Ashley established a Ministry Training School in the Solomon Islands from which hundreds of men and women pioneered new churches across South Pacific island nations.

Called by God to train people in Europe, in 1993 Ashley was filled afresh with God's Spirit and moved with his family to Britain. As the Holy Spirit moved, a new church was rapidly established in Brighton. Men and women were soon trained and sent out across Britain, founding many new churches. Ashley continues to train leaders across Eastern and Western Europe, the Middle East and Asia.

Scores of Christian leaders now call Ashley their spiritual father, because he trained them personally by imparting both God's word and life's principles. Thousands more have had their lives impacted during decades of ministering across diverse countries and cultures.

Ashley has been a part of several distinctive moves of God's Spirit, seeing many amazing miracles. He is a real pioneer who communicates with humour and a deep love for God.

In January 2009 Ashley was appointed as International President of Christian Outreach Centre and today works strategically with national church leaders across most continents of the world. Ashley lives to help people fulfil their God-given destiny and reach many with the good news of Jesus Christ.

What others say about
Fruit for Eternity

Ashley Schmierer hits home with his book on life lessons learned. Expressed in a form that is light hearted, easy to grasp and hard to put down, this is a MUST-READ for all who want practical tips on leadership, ministry and life.

Kong Hee – President, City Harvest Church, Singapore

Ashley Schmierer's call to bear 'fruit for eternity' is an inspiring, encouraging and challenging story. From the rugged farmlands of Queensland to the spiritual harvest fields of the South Pacific Islands, Africa and Europe, Ashley's journey has produced a wealth of spiritual experience which he passes on to others. The book is not just a biographical record of God's dealings with Ashley and his family, but it is also peppered with vital principles applicable to us all. Ashley and his team are doing sterling work for the Lord in Brighton and beyond. Here is one man who not only 'talks the talk' but also demonstrates the fruit of faith and passionate labour for the Lord. I wholeheartedly commend the book and the ministry it represents.

Colin Dye – Senior Pastor, Kensington Temple,
London City Church, London, UK

If you want to be inspired to live an extraordinary life, read *Fruit for Eternity*. Your dreams will be forever stirred to do something great for God. Once you start reading this book, you won't put it down.

Brian Klemmer – Klemmer & Associates, Leadership & Character Development Company, USA

Ashley and I go back a long way and we have experienced many amazing times together. I know this book will be a great read for many. It will encourage you to dig into God's word and find for yourself, as Ashley has, a journey that will take you beyond anything you could ever imagine. I know Ashley's heart in writing this book is to help people break free from the limitations they put on themselves. Well done, Ash!

Neil Miers – Former International President, Christian Outreach Centre

I thank God that I was given the privilege of being one of Ashley's 'father's in the faith', and also the opportunity to see this Aussie man become transformed by the grace of God from a farmer to a man of faith for the nations of the world. Because of this dramatic change of lifestyle, I am sure his story and insights will inspire many to believe in the God who does the impossible through ordinary people. Ashley, you've done me proud to see the grace man of God that you have become.

Kevin Dales – Senior Minister, Christian Outreach Centre, Adelaide, Australia

I love Ashley Schmierer! He's a man of faith and has seen more happen through his ministry in a few years than some see in a lifetime. This book is highlights of his experiences. It is a why and how book all at the same time. He tells you why he believes, preaches, acts and works as hard as he does. It is also a book of how, with insightful and helpful tips on subjects from marriage to mission trips. Read this and enjoy the rollercoaster ride of one of God's great ministers.

Scott Wilson – President, Eurolead.net and ICLM, Denmark

In this book my dear friend, Ashley Schmierer, details his upbringing, early encounters with God, his dream and humble beginnings in the ministry. I have found his testimony to be educational, inspiring, encouraging, humorous and life changing! The thought provoking tips and nuggets for ministry that he shares in this book have impacted my life as a leader. I could hardly put the book down, except for occasions where I had to pause for brief moments to reflect on what I had read. This testimony has not only challenged me, but has also inspired and encouraged me to pursue and fulfil my God-given dream, just like Ashley did. This book must definitely be on the bookshelf of every believer and in every church leader's study.

Ben C. Ndobe – Apostle, Dominion Life Cathedral,
Tembisa, Kempton Park, South Africa

Ashley, it's a pity that you didn't work on your French better at school, but now I have to make an effort to speak English. I thank God for the divine appointment and the ongoing connection we have with you. You and Ruth have been such a great help for our family and for the church. Thank you for taking us under your wing and continuing to lead us today.

Marie Pons (formerly Biville) – COC Dunkerque, France

Ashley is a good friend and a source of great inspiration in my life. I know that, as you read this book, he will become one of yours too. Ashley loves God and His church passionately. He is a spiritual leader and true father in the faith. His life demonstrates that he is not a mere seated believer, but indeed a walking disciple and daily follower of Jesus. Join him on a journey of faith that will take you around the world – a story of a life well lived, jammed full of nuggets and wisdom for those wanting to live impacting lives; a story of faith and overcoming that will inspire you to reach for all that God has for you.

Andy Elmes – Senior Minister,
Portsmouth Family Church, UK

Having had the privilege of walking with Ashley from the beginning of his ministry, I have seen what God can accomplish through a man willing to surrender his will to the Father's will. Ashley has written a transparent account of his encounters with God, while depositing on paper the wisdom he has learned and applied successfully. Ashley is a true modern-day apostle who inspires all believers and challenges unbelievers with the gospel, while causing demons to flee from strongholds. *Fruit for Eternity* is inspirational.

Chas Gullo – Doctor/Senior Pastor, Suncoast Church,
Christian Outreach Centre, Woombye, Australia

I have known Ashley Schmierer for many years and consider him a dynamic and yet humble servant of God with a truly apostolic fire burning in his heart. I have seen the outstanding fruit of his ministry in the churches and leaders Ashley has mentored. He and his wife have truly helped transform thousands of lives. With a unique Aussie flavour, Ashley imparts courage and faith to believe for great things from our God. This book is a story of a true trail blazer. I pray you catch the special fire this servant of God carries.

Mahesh Chavda – Senior Pastor,
All Nations Church, Charlotte, NC, USA

I believe that, as you read the inspiring stories of Ashley's life and ministry, you will marvel at the work of God in the life of an ordinary man. A man who has willingly yielded to the Master's hand and been lifted to heights he could have never hoped for or dreamed possible. You will be encouraged. You will be strengthened. You will find Ashley's practical, proven points on various topics very helpful. It is my great honour to know Ashley and Ruth as friends and fellow partners in serving God's plans and purposes for His Church.

Robert Maasbach – Senior Pastor, Life Church,
Folkestone, UK

I believe in the power of the Holy Spirit working effectively in a person's life! When I first met my husband, Ashley, he was a hard-working, well-meaning man who loved God, but was unable to share God's love with other people. However, an encounter with the Spirit of God forged in Ashley a radical change of heart that filled him with compassion for his fellow man. Over the decades, we have walked together through floods and droughts, joy and tears, mountains and valleys, year by year, nation by nation, seeing God's powerful love reach multitudes of people. Prepare to be touched by God's Spirit, as you enjoy reading *Fruit for Eternity.*

Ruth Schmierer – Ashley's wife, Co-President,
Christian Outreach Centre

Contents

Dedication

This book is dedicated to the women who have influenced my life:

Miriam Schmierer, my Grandma, who lived to be the oldest person in Australia. Her positive attitude to life has been a constant inspiration.

Lily Dales, my British-born Grandma, whose birth certificate allowed me to move with my family to the United Kingdom.

Joan, my mother. You are always there for me and have been a friend through difficult times, especially after losing Pop. Thank you for praying with me and believing in the call of God upon my life. You are the best mother a son could ever want.

Melonie, my daughter, who is unique, certainly someone special and the only one of your kind. You are so smart, but most of all, thank you for your friendship, your support and for telling me that I was the best preacher.

Amy, my daughter, who has such an inner strength of leadership, intuitive wisdom and thoughtfulness towards others. You have a sharp wit, are so intelligent and a real achiever. Thank you for always being a great friend.

And most of all, *Ruth*, my amazing wife and lifelong friend. It's been an exciting life so far and I couldn't have done much in my life without you. You were a preacher long before I was, and inspired me by your love and commitment to the cause. You now travel the nations being a true mother in the gospel and are the wisest, kindest person I have ever met. Thank you for standing with me in the dream.

Foreword

When Paul the apostle first encountered Jesus on the road to Damascus, he asked two important questions. The first was, "Who are You, Lord?" and the second, "What is it You want me to do?" The answer he received was a mandate to build, establish and expand the Kingdom of God. I believe this continues to be the mandate of God to people today.

I have known Ashley since he first came to the United Kingdom from Australia with Ruth and their family and, throughout that time, I have found him to be a man completely focused on the same mission as Paul in 'seeking first the Kingdom of God.'

Ashley's vision has continually expanded from a small town in north Queensland, Australia, across the South Pacific to the UK, Middle East, India and now to encompass the whole globe. His greatest gift is to provoke and catalyze people to fulfilling the plans and purposes of God – the 'good works that God has prepared beforehand' for their lives.

Other than my family, he has been and continues to be the single most influential figure in my life. We have laughed together and cried together, been through good times and sad times. Whatever the situation, he has faced it with tenacity, courage, determination and faith that God will give him the breakthrough.

What follows is an account of some of the events of his life, and I encourage you to let yourself be inspired by Ashley's example of what God can do through a man who surrenders to the Kingdom mandate.

David Harland – Senior Pastor, CityCoast Church, Christian Outreach Centre Brighton & Hove, United Kingdom

Introduction

Jesus said,

> *"By this My Father is glorified, that you bear much fruit; so also you will be My disciples."*
>
> (John 15:8)

I will forever remember the night, I first heard God's voice, "If you follow Me, you will have fruit for eternity." At that time I was a fruit grower and knew well the principles of producing fruit.

Throughout this book I tell my story and some of what I've learned along the way.

Here are steps and keys that I would have liked to have known when I started on my journey. Sometimes, we just want to know what to do and how to do it. I have learned a lot from great leaders and friends, and other keys I have discovered myself.

The greatest key has been recognising and obeying the voice of the Holy Spirit.

Jesus also said,

> *"The harvest is truly plentiful, but the labourers are few. Therefore pray the Lord of the harvest to send out labourers into His harvest."* (Matthew 9:37-38)

I pray that, as you read this book, it will inspire and help you towards fruitfulness in your life.

Everyone has value, everyone can be fruitful, and everyone matters to God. As you rise and develop in God's plan for your life, make sure you take others with you.

1 *It Really Was A Ghost*

Where did Grandad go every afternoon? Each day at almost the same time Grandad broke a small branch from a bush near the corner of our farm house and quietly walked down towards the trees by the gully. A gully is a small valley gouged out by the rare but strong storm waters. Grandad flicked the branch over his shoulder as he walked, dislodging the stubborn flies. Anyone who has been in the Australian bush will know that flies will settle on any living thing that moves. Grandad never looked back, and it seemed to me as though he was going somewhere special. As I was ten years old and very inquisitive, one day I followed him at a distance.

Grandad, my mother's father, came most years to visit us on our family farm at Gayndah, south-east Queensland, Australia. A tall man with broad shoulders, blue eyes and a welcoming smile, he had a memorable turn of phrase. Once looking at my big feet, he said, "If you didn't crawl along the ground so far, you would have been a bit taller." Reflecting on modern financial opportunities, he would shake his head and say, "If I was young now, I could make so much money a kangaroo couldn't jump over it."

I was extremely proud of Grandad. Once he showed me his scars where a bullet had gone in his shoulder and out the other side, when he was fighting as a volunteer for the

Allies in France during World War I. He had survived the Battle of the Somme but was shot in the following battle, at Amiens. From that time on I thought, "Grandad is tough. Even a bullet couldn't kill him!" Milking the cows together one morning, he shouted to me, "Ashley, your Queen and country needs you!" I straightened up and thought about it. 'Does the Queen really need me?' I thought about the Queen, living in a castle far away in England. To a small boy on an Australian farm, England was a land impossibly far away, full of kings and queens and mysterious traditions.

That day, as Grandad walked down to the trees by the gully, I kept my distance. He sat on a rock overlooking the gully with his back towards me. It didn't seem terribly exciting, so I decided to sneak up and jump on him. Grandad was such fun that I knew he would see the funny side of it. Dead leaves on the ground crackled under my feet as I tried to tread quietly. A few metres away I heard noise. Was Grandad talking and singing to himself? I stopped in my tracks as I strained to listen.

Suddenly, I sensed something invisible beside me! Whatever it was shocked me and even frightened me, because it felt like a ghost. Grandad had not realised I was behind him and was still singing, but I knew I had to get away as fast as I could. Stepping backwards, I retraced my footsteps to avoid making a noise and getting his attention. Then I ran for my life. Back in my bedroom with my heart pounding, I resolved never to sneak up on Grandad again. I did not believe in ghosts, but what had happened caused me to wonder. Many years later, I remembered this experience and realised it was my first encounter with the Holy Ghost.

I realised Grandad went down to the gully each day for solitude and to pray. If I had known it was God, maybe I would not have run away but would have gone to ask Grandad about my experience. There was no doubt about it

– Grandad had more than a nodding acquaintance with God. In his younger years as Pastor Samuel Dales, my Grandad had founded three churches in North Queensland.

Pop and Mum were very busy with farm duties in the mornings, so a friend from town, Mr Morris, would drive out to the farm and collect the Schmierer tribe for Sunday school. He had been a missionary to Sudan in his younger years. I can still hear this dry old chap asking if we knew our memory verses but most times he got the same answer, "No, Mr Morris!" I came to really appreciate the great sacrifice of this man, giving the time each week to drive us children to Sunday school.

Long Sunday school and church services felt like an eternity to an outdoor, adventure seeking farm boy. I spent most services thumbing through the back pages of my Bible, examining maps of Paul's missionary journeys to pass the time. I envied the Apostle Paul's life, and thought wistfully, "It was interesting for Paul, going to all these places, but me, I have to sit here in this boring church." I sang every second verse of the hymns, just to feel as though I was doing something different and to make life a bit more interesting.

Writing this book, I have now travelled to many places on St Paul's ministry journeys such as Ephesus, Rome and Salamis, and have helped train people and establish churches in Malta and Damascus. I often think of those Sundays fidgeting and fighting boredom on hard pews. It matters not where you start in life but where you finish. Life really is exciting when you obey the call of God!

2 *The Early Years*

My home town of Gayndah, a four hour drive north-west of Brisbane, is the oldest town in Queensland and was once considered for the state capital. 'Gayndah' meant 'place of thunder' in the local Aboriginal language. I loved watching the lightning in the night sky and hearing the thunder that would rumble for many hours in the summer nights. The Aborigines had named Gayndah well. I always liked that I was born at a 'place of thunder.' A dramatic place for an entrance into this world!

Gayndah, positioned on the banks of the Burnett River, is a sleepy little town with a steady 1,800 residents. Like most country towns of Australia it has a very close knit community and, although it isn't actually considered gossip, you eventually find out everything about everyone.

The oldest son in a family of six children, I had three older sisters and a younger brother and sister. My parents, Austin and Joan, ensured that we attended Sunday school and gave us a good home life, encouraging us to stay on the straight and narrow. Mum kept an eye on our spiritual life and occasionally came and prayed with me when I went to bed. Pop and Mum were people of integrity and successful dairy farmers. We worked and loved the farm life and, as kids, always checked on each other that all were doing their share of the jobs. If anyone slacked, Mum would be told for sure, and the ultimate threat was to tell Pop!

In the late 1960's Pop bought a Ford Falcon GT that was the envy of the town. Nick-named Moonshine, as a younger man he had a reputation as a bit of a dare-devil and would ride into town standing on the seat of his 1000cc motorbike. In the night, as he sped along the road, people said he looked like a ray of moonshine through the trees.

As a boy I watched Pop's friend, Bertie Buettel, driving his horse and buggy and parking in the main street. Gayndah, like other country towns, has a very wide main street, not for the busy traffic but designed for a horse and dray to turn around. By this time the horses and drays were disappearing – but not Bertie's. As he parked his horse and buggy next to all the cars, I wondered why he didn't get a car like everyone else. One day, while standing on the footpath, I thought, "Maybe Bertie just doesn't want to change." It was this thought that later inspired me to learn to email and use a Blackberry. I didn't want to end up like Bertie myself, left behind in a bygone era just because I didn't want to change.

Pop often taught me the principles of maintaining machinery and how to run the farm. He was always right, witty and fun to be with. When I was twelve, Pop called me out of the house, laid a hessian bag on the ground under the truck and said, "It is time you learnt how to grease the truck." 'Yuk,' I thought as I looked at my hands, 'this is so dirty and sticky.' But I nodded gravely. Pop was giving me a man's job to do – a lesson in how to be a man – and it made me feel very grown up. A short time later, when we sold that truck, I watched as Pop took the potential buyer around the truck and told him all the things that were wrong with it. As the man walked around the other side, I whispered to Pop, "What are you doing? The guy won't buy it now!" Pop just said, "Wait and see." Later that afternoon we stood together and watched as the truck was driven down the road with the same contented buyer at the wheel. I decided this was a second lesson in how to be a man.

We had a flood one year and the gullies were awash with storm water from the dams overflowing. I caught some wild ducks, brought them home, made a special pen for them and asked Pop to get me some cement, because I was going to make a big pond for them. I dug the hole and started mixing my concrete. To my surprise Pop came and started to help me. I hadn't asked him or even expected him to. After all, it was my idea and Pop was busy with all the big farming jobs. We were kneeling over the hole and patting the concrete up the walls of my duck pond when I looked up into my father's face. I thought, 'You could be doing a lot of things today, but you are here helping me do what I want to do.' It's strange that I remember this event over forty years later, but it is similar to how God wants to help us through life. I guess God is fairly busy, but He really does care about helping and likes to be around us.

One year the sale yard cattle prices were very high and Pop asked me, "If you were running the farm, what would you do?" Looking at the high prices, I decided, "Sell all the cattle." But Pop smiled and said, "What would you use for breeders for the next year?" While I had my eye on the quick money, Pop was thinking of the long term.

One Saturday we were making a bench in the shed and I felt it was taking up too much of my day. As I worked hastily, Pop looked at my shoddy work and quoted words I would remember for the rest of my life: "If a job's worth doing, it's worth doing well!"

Tips for parents

→ Take an interest in what each child is doing in his/her life.

→ Teach them to work.

→ Share your heart with each child, individually.

→ Be an example.

→ Regularly pray for each child.

→ Never compare one child with another.

→ Let each child know that you are proud of them for who they are and not just for what they achieve.

→ Be consistent and in agreement with your partner regarding discipline.

→ Always encourage your children to be involved in a good church.

→ Speak positive words about others in front of your children. Avoid negative words that breed cynicism.

→ Have fun with your children.

At school, outsmarting my teachers and at thirteen years having my name listed as the 'class clown' in the school magazine felt like the pinnacle of achievement. However all too many evenings were spent sitting at my desk, writing out thousands of times, 'I must behave in school'. One night Pop came into my room and saw me writing with five pens taped together so as to only do one-fifth of the work. He stared at me thoughtfully and said, "What do you think your teacher is doing at this moment?" I said, "Umm, probably watching television." Pop responded, "You think you've won, but tomorrow night she will be watching television again while you write more lines." That night I realised that my teacher was the one who was winning and I was actually losing. That was the last time I ever had to write out lines. Pop always had the right words to point out when I was too much of a smart aleck to see the big picture.

"Schmierer, it is a good thing that there are some towns in Western Queensland that don't yet have a sewerage system!" my teacher shouted. "You will be carrying out the poo buckets." Our manual arts teacher was feared by all students. He had once made a fellow student sweep the whole woodwork room with a toothbrush. I dared not answer back, but immediately decided that this boy was not going to be carrying out any poo buckets!

Thirty-seven years later I was visiting my mother in Gayndah when she said, "There's a dinner on in a nearby hall and some people will be there whom you have not seen for many years. Would you like to come along with me?" I decided it would be good to reconnect with old acquaintances. "Sure Mum, I'll go with you," I replied.

As I entered the hall, I noticed that the gathering was mostly older farmers and I recognised many faces. There he was, my old manual arts teacher, greying and much frailer than the fearsome teacher of my memories. I quietly sat next to him and thought carefully about what to say. "Sir, you were wrong." He turned his head and slowly asked, "How was I wrong?" With clear intention I explained the paths my life had taken, and that carrying poo buckets had not been among them!

In his early years Pop attended a Brethren church and Mum was brought up in an Assemblies of God church. I'm not sure how we came to be Baptist, but they might have thought it was a good 'middle of the road' church for bringing up the kids. Regularly on Sunday nights, my mother would take us to the local Assemblies of God church. All I remember was hearing that Jesus was coming back and we needed to be ready to meet Him, because He might come back before dawn.

At fourteen years of age, one Sunday night I had already decided that after Pastor Erikson preached, I would do something I knew had to be done. As usual, he gave an invitation for those who wanted to receive Christ to come to the front and say a prayer to ask God for forgiveness. Determined to do it, and having imagined this moment in my mind, I slipped to the end of the pew and made my way down the aisle to the front of the church. Although someone else also came forward that night, I was glad to be first. It was the right thing to do, to get it out of the way so I wouldn't go to hell. It must have taken a lot for my mother to take us to church on those Sunday nights, and I thank God for parents who pay that price for the sake of their children.

When I was sixteen years of age, my pastor announced that there would be a water baptism the following week, so I asked if he would baptise me. "Why do you want to be water baptised?" he quizzed me. "Because Jesus was baptised in water and the Bible tells us to," I replied, hoping that I would satisfy my enquiring pastor. With a nod and friendly smile he responded, "You have answered well." I was glad to have passed the pastor's test, and the following week was baptised in water at our local church, along with several others.

Looking for opportunities to make money was always in my blood. Raising hundreds of turkeys for sale at Christmas time was a really profitable venture. Another time, I asked Pop to plough up all the area around the house for my market garden. Always looking for some profit, I managed to sell the deformed or grub-eaten vegetables to Mum at half price, while all the good ones were sold in the local shops.

In May 1971 our farm was overwhelmed by a plague of mice. The wet season usually kept the mouse population in check, but that year the rain didn't arrive, and huge numbers of mice spread into our barns, looking for food. Pop used various pest control techniques to rid the barns and sheds of the vermin, but noting the vastness of this mouse plague, I asked Pop if he would pay me one cent per mouse and I would be his man rather than the uncertain results of the pest company. I began catching mice that Saturday afternoon, and within hours I presented Pop with a bucket full of dead mice (catching mice and releasing them outdoors is not a sensible option during a mouse plague), and I think that he started wondering just what he had agreed to. The next day at High School my mates laughed and said, "Schmierer, we couldn't be bothered to catch a mouse for one cent." Over the next few months, I devised scores of plans to catch mice. On the cold winter mornings I would find dozens of them huddled under hessian bags. Grabbing them with my bare hands, stomping on them and setting dozens of various mouse traps, my tally of dead mice rapidly grew. A bottle greased with butter, protruding from a bale of hay with a piece of melted cheese in the neck was one successful strategy. Underneath was a tub of water to catch the mice who tried in vain to eat the cheese, only to slip on the greasy bottle into the water and drown. The ideas came thick and fast and thousands of mice were caught each week.

At fifteen years of age, on the Friday before the August school term holidays, a school mate asked, "Ash, whatcha doin' during the holidays?" "A coach trip through central Australia with all expenses paid – all through catching mice," I replied. Over a few months, tens of thousands of the vermin had been caught. Pop was happy and so was I. I employed my sister, Pam, to look after my mice business while I was travelling, on a fifty percent share basis. Sadly for my business, the plague eventually came to an end but there was always another opportunity to make money.

Pop had kept bee hives for many years and on weekends we often tended them together. Sometimes, a hobby becomes a job. Slowly we added to our hives until there were over a hundred bee hives which took up a lot of our spare time. It was something that Pop and I did together. He taught me how to find a wild bee hive in a tree by tracking bees from where they were drinking water. We would cut the tree down, find the queen bee and add the hive to our collection. Pop was very good at spotting a hive in a tree. Once we were driving along a road at 100 km per hour, not even looking for bee hives, when he pointed and said, "There's a bee hive! I just saw the sun shining on the wings of the bees as they entered that tree." We turned around to check, and sure enough Pop was right.

We had all of the bee-keeping equipment and in one season took three tons of honey from our bees. This we sold at various local shops. The bees were very vicious and, if the gauze veil over my face was not positioned right, I would be stung repeatedly until I could fix the veil. One night Mum found seventeen bee stings in my neck.

I made an observation bee hive for my bedroom that had clear Perspex on each side and a long, enclosed entrance which led up to the window. Many evenings, instead of doing my homework, I sat watching my bees.

3 *The Pain Won't Always Be This Much*

We would wash our socks and hang them out to dry on the handlebars. My sister and I had great plans for a trip around Australia by motorbike. I was aged eighteen and feeling somewhat restless, and we were looking to chill out and travel. Pop didn't think it was such a good idea and quizzed me on how I would protect my sister, if necessary. Crestfallen, I confessed, "Pop, that was the farthest thing from my mind!"

We chose the far less stressful alternative for worried parents and went to a Brethren youth camp at Hervey Bay. Pop always had a way of turning me around and this time I was very glad he did.

As it happened, meeting the love of my life was far better than a trip around Australia on a motorbike. After a few days at the youth camp, a game of winks and a vision in a pink bikini, I thought it was time to make a move. A man has to know when to make that move – not too quick and definitely not too slow!

Sitting around the tables at the camp, I launched my only chat up line, as only a farmer looking for a wife can do. "Where do you toil?" I asked. Ruth looked somewhat bemused and replied, "I don't." I didn't know what to make of that, and was relieved when she explained that she was going to college for teacher training.

A few days later, Ruth told me she'd had a dream about us. This was very good news. Apart from my sisters, the only other girl in our church youth group was rather overweight. I had spent several years worrying that I would have to marry her, by default. Now a brown-haired lass in a pink bikini had a dream about me! I thought this was rather cool but it did scare me a bit. My dreams were more like nightmares. Several times as a boy, I woke in the night thinking communists had surrounded our farm house! At that time, Australian troops were fighting in Vietnam, so growing up I wondered if one day it could be me on the battlefield. I was comforted by Mum's words that, because of my knobbly knees, the army might reject me! A few decades later I have preached in the Ukraine under the hammer and sickle emblem, alongside a good friend who had been a former atheist, Russian colonel. That same man later told me he was once in a meeting where strategies for the invasion of Australia were discussed.

Three months after meeting Ruth, my world would change forever. One day in March 1975, Pop was taken to hospital with vomiting and severe headaches. That day I had worked with him on the farm when he said that something was wrong and he didn't have much strength in one hand. Visiting Pop in hospital was not a sight that any of us were used to, as he was always strong and seldom got sick. After many tests and only a few weeks, the doctors diagnosed a serious brain tumour which required an urgent operation. Pop never regained consciousness and a few days later on the 18th of April 1975, he tragically and unexpectedly died.

My father's funeral was huge for our country town. He was well known and liked by everyone, both for his good character and dry wit. Our German ancestors were some of the first four settlers in the Gayndah district and Pop, or

'Austie' Schmierer as he was known, had passed away at only forty-nine years of age.

As is the custom, after the funeral some friends and relatives came back to our house for a snack afterwards. It was difficult and some were sitting at the kitchen table trying to make conversation. As I opened the fly screen door and took a few steps into the kitchen, I heard one of my uncles give an awkward chuckle.

How could they laugh in our house when Pop had just died and been buried today? I was angry and confused and felt like evicting everyone from our house, but instead walked awkwardly past them to my bedroom and closed the door. I lay down with my face in the pillow and for the first time cried about losing Pop. Pop was not just my father but my friend, workmate and boss. Being the eldest son, I felt the weight of responsibility that was now upon me. I was angry. It was not fair. I couldn't imagine our family without Pop. Whatever were we going to do? We had two farms and now the cattle prices had crashed. The prices were so low that some farmers were shooting cattle rather than selling them at the markets. The cattle prices would not even cover the freight to the markets.

I heard my bedroom door open but did not look up. Someone put a hand on my shoulder and said, "Ash, the pain won't always be this much." I recognised the voice as that of my father's best friend, Kevin Dales. Kevin was also a farmer who would later be called into ministry and establish the Innisfail Christian Outreach Centre church in North Queensland. Kevin's kind action came to have enormous significance to me. Eight years later Kevin would train me for the ministry and, in so doing, become my 'father in the Lord.' On the day that my natural father was buried, it was Kevin who noticed me missing and came to put his hand on my shoulder.

Pop and I had been good friends, not just father and son. I felt the weight of responsibility to run our two farms and help my mother raise the two younger children. Kerry, Marcia and Pam, my three older sisters, now had jobs and lives of their own, but Tommy was twelve and Lynny was only five. The night after the funeral, Lynny and I were looking at the stars and she asked me, "When is Daddy coming back?" I was nineteen and this was all too much. How could I tell her that Daddy was not coming back? The words kept repeating in my head, as I told myself, 'You have to be Daddy now.' Such a weight had now fallen upon my shoulders. Later that night I sat on the outside steps of our farmhouse and heard Mum crying in the bedroom. I wanted to run and leave the responsibility behind me. How did it end up like this? It wasn't fair. I could hear another voice within that was calling me to carry it all like a man. Pop had trained me to be that man.

The following weeks were very difficult for us all, and it was a matter of taking one day at a time. Walking down the street of our small town, I saw a person who knew our family well coming towards me. When this man saw me, he crossed to the other side of the street. I felt hurt that he had ignored me. How strange people are, that we avoid a person because we don't know what to say.

Mum showed exceptional strength, and later also ran for local government and was elected. She served as councillor for twenty-one years and received an outstanding award for her service, being one of the longest serving women in Queensland's local government.

Soon after meeting Ruth, I went to visit her in Brisbane where she was training as a primary and pre-school teacher. She told me of an exciting new church that had begun in that city. I thought, 'I have never seen an exciting church, so let's go have a look.' It was unlike any church I'd ever seen, with people swaying and waving their hands in the air. I decided that although the people there looked happy, there'd clearly been booze or drugs before the meeting and possibly more afterwards. The end of the service could not come too soon, and as we walked away I said to Ruth, "If you are going to be my wife, I don't want you going back to that place." This was our first visit to a Christian Outreach Centre church and would be the last for seven more years. I certainly didn't expect that, many years later, God would entrust me to become the International President of the Christian Outreach Centre movement of churches. God sure does have a sense of humour!

Ruth and I were married on the 17th of December 1977 on our own farm, Mount Debatable, as soon as Ruth completed her training as a teacher. Our property was called Mount Debatable because the mountain nearby was where the early settlers met to debate the various plots of land that each would farm.

It was so good to have rescued Ruth from that crazy church and the big city. We settled into life at Gayndah where there were certainly no churches like that!

Tips for marriage

→ *Don't marry someone because you are lonely, but rather because you love them just as they are. Never marry someone thinking that you will change them.*

→ *Always be best friends. Recognise and adjust quickly if ever this seems to wane.*

→ *Give tender loving care into the relationship and never be just a taker.*

→ *Accept that your partner will probably have a different personality type to yours. Accept that he/she will see things from a different angle than you do and this is a great asset.*

→ *Understand each other. Don't let your mind dwell on the little things that irritate you. Remember that we all have our idiosyncrasies.*

→ *Give each other space.*

→ *Listen to advice from your partner who knows you well.*

→ *Talk about anything and everything. Learn how to talk about heart issues and find the way to do this without irritating each other.*

→ *Don't pretend. Keep no secrets from each other. Listen to the heart, not merely to words. Look for the appropriate time for deep communication.*

→ *Don't gossip with friends about your relationship.*

→ *Never mock or scoff but always give honour to your partner.*

→ *If love ever seems to decrease, remember that love is far more than a feeling. Love is a commitment.*

→ *One of the greatest tests of a marriage is to always forgive and keep no records.*

→ *If your partner is offended or hurt by someone else, never take on the offence yourself. Help and pray for your partner through their difficulty.*

→ *Establish the habit of budgeting in your finances and allow for holidays together.*

→ *Always remember that trust is earned and can never be demanded.*

→ *Appreciate the privilege of living together and make life fun.*

After Ruth and I were married, I would spend long days on my tractor, ploughing the soil while thinking about life and the future. One day the thought came to me while ploughing, 'I don't want to get to heaven and regret this life.' I pondered on and was motivated by this thought for decades to come, and it has helped me to keep an eternal focus to my life.

Our first year of married life did not go entirely smoothly. Ruth had to adjust to living in a small farming town, married to a farmer who would track mud through previously spotless bathrooms and bed sheets. I, in turn, had to adjust to life with a friendly woman who loved meeting people and socialising when I was much happier in the silence and solitude of nature.

Ruth's brother was always talking about the church, Christian Outreach Centre, and miracles that were apparently happening there. His visits to our farm were not something I looked forward to. Keeping away from him was the weekend plan but, as I was driving the tractor into our shed to refill seed for planting, I saw my brother-in-law walking towards the shed. Eager as he was, this called for some quick thinking to outsmart him. As I jumped off the tractor, I kept it in neutral and revving loudly, just to avoid his chatter of COC, miracles and the like. As he shouted into my ear about healings and miracles, I put down the seed and turned to him, "Don't tell me about miracles that are hundreds of miles away. Do one now in front of me!" I felt I had won this round. As Ruth stood smiling and waved her family goodbye, I bared my teeth in the semblance of a smile and thought, 'Glad to see the end of you and your miracles.' But God had already started to reel me in.

"You will know when God calls you," the man said. When I was a boy, a missionary from Papua New Guinea had come to our Baptist church. He came with stories of the mission, slides of huts and topless tribal ladies, and mention of this mysterious 'call'. The thought would cross my mind for many of the following years. 'How will I know, because I can't see or hear Him?'

4 *Do You Think You Are Moses?*

||||||||||||||||||||||||||||||||||||||||||||||||||||||||||||||||||||||||||||||||||||||||||||||||||||||||||||||||||||||||||||||||||||||||||||||

"What do you want most in your life?" one of the leaders of the Wesleyan Methodist Bible study asked our prayer group. I was contemplating rain for my crops, a good life, wealth... But all these great thoughts were cut short when Ruth spoke out, "I would like to hear God's voice speaking to me." I was so embarrassed that my materialistic thoughts of greatness seemed to evaporate. When it was my turn, I had nothing to say and just muttered "Pass!" As we got in the car to go home, I provoked Ruth, "Do you think you are Moses? Why would God speak to you? Do you think He is going to come down in some burning bush just for you?"

One Sunday in church I spent an entire sermon watching a caterpillar progress outside the church foyer, wondering if it would reach safety before the preacher finished his sermon. On several occasions I sensed the sermon drawing to a close and feared for the life of the adventurous caterpillar. At the close of the sermon the caterpillar was safe but, as I looked across at Ruth and saw tears in her eyes, I realised I had missed a crucial part of the message.

In the Wesleyan church our pastor wept as he shared his heart for people and I was quite moved that someone could feel so deeply, because really I didn't think much about people. In the first year of married life, Ruth often invited people to our house. When this happened I would complain,

"Sweetheart, I have chosen you from all the women of the world. I don't want anyone else, why can't you just be happy with me?"

Ruth got involved in the children's work and both of us in the youth leadership of the Wesleyan church. We enjoyed being a part of this small family church and it seemed like the perfect place to come and do a little, but not too much.

To be on the roster to take communion emblems to the people was a big honour and one week I was chosen for this task. I studied in detail the men who did it the week before, paying special attention to their walk, facial expressions and general demeanour. In our bathroom I practised how to walk and pause as someone took the bread and wine, while at the same time glancing in the mirror to make sure my face had an appropriately solemn expression. The other men had a particularly reverent way of standing, with their mouths drooping at the edges into an upside down U.

On the day all went according to plan and I felt so good and pleased with myself. I was first to the car to wait for Ruth and anticipated some praise, such as "I was so proud of you" or "You looked so holy." Instead, Ruth looked at me and said, "Why did you look like that?" Puzzled, I asked, "Like what?" She answered, "You looked like you had a pain." I explained, "That is how they all look." It was the end of my explaining, but inside I was discouraged as I pondered, "I could not even please Ruth, so how could I have pleased God?"

I noticed that preachers' hands were soft as though they never worked. They didn't seem to live a very exciting life, mainly visiting people, having cups of coffee and shaking people's hands at the door of the church. One day I was working on the farm and saw from a distance the preacher's car coming down our road. I thought, 'Oh no, hasn't he got anything better to do? He'll waste at least two hours of my time!' The preacher would come by, spouting encouraging Bible verses at inconvenient hours when I needed to work.

I was passionate about the land and about all that could be accomplished. I hired bulldozers to clear the trees, formed many contour banks to stop erosion, planted various crops and extended our irrigation system.

Once I went to our local preacher and asked him whether he thought that I would one day leave the farm and go into full-time ministry. He asked, "Has God called you now?" I replied, "No." He continued, "Well, keep doing what you are doing." I was relieved by his word to me, because I loved the farm and its dirt. At times when I was ploughing, I felt like rolling in the freshly upturned soil. Strange as it sounds, this is how much I loved being a farmer.

Planting a citrus orchard was my next step. Firstly, in a nursery I raised thousands of young trees which I then grafted and planted out in the paddock. In the year before I sold the farm, we installed seven kilometres of underground irrigation pipes to water those trees with trickle irrigation. I was very passionate about being a successful farmer and it was my dream until God called me into the ministry.

Reluctantly, I began to do preaching in the local Wesleyan Methodist church, but this was more my pastor's idea rather than mine. I would sometimes practise preaching to Ruth, as she prepared our dinner, by standing at the other end of the kitchen with my notes on the deep freezer. My sermon was written down word for word and Ruth would say, "Smile a little as you say that." Also, at another point, "You need to emphasise those words more." I wrote in large red letters 'smile' and 'emphasise' at various places through my sermon notes. The flow of public speaking did not come easily, as I was not a gifted speaker. I was an extremely self-conscious person who had managed to avoid making speeches all throughout my secondary school years.

The pastor once asked me to pray publicly in the church the following week. I wrote down the prayer and during the week memorized it. Desperately wanting to do my best, I grasped the prayer in sweating hands as I stood behind the lectern. I was so nervous that I could not even connect my eyes, mouth and mind with the words that I had written. Walking away, I thought, 'What a fool I have made of myself!' Never again did I want to speak or pray publicly.

Most people think their in-laws are rather strange but Herb, my father-in-law, was certainly a little eccentric. Although Herb was handy at fixing anything, he was so different from my straight farming upbringing and, to say the least, there was the usual undercurrent of friction when he came.

On one occasion, he came to visit us on a motorbike towing a trailer and caused a few looks in town. He was, to put it mildly, rather different.

As I looked at the afternoon sky, I knew time was going to be tight to get the hay baled and all in the shed before the rain came. I was out on the tractor and mostly finished baling, when I noticed my new one ton truck being driven onto the paddock. It didn't take long for me to see that Herb was driving it, because he quickly got out and put two bales on the back of the truck. Then he drove up to another hay bale, stopped and proceeded to put it on the bonnet or hood, then put another next to it. How he thought he was going to drive I will never know, because it totally blocked his vision from the driving seat. I was livid. Jumping off the tractor, I shouted, "Look what you have done! Are you stupid?" Back at the house, I insisted that Ruth come to see what her father had done to my new truck. With a flashlight I made sure Ruth saw the scratches on the bonnet and then she became very quiet.

Next morning I woke early and left to do more work in the far paddock. To my relief, I saw Herb riding away on his motor bike, trailer in tow. On my return home, Ruth was still very quiet and somewhat sad as she slowly spoke, "Dad will not be coming back." She paused, then continued, "He has gone but, before he did, he said you were making the same mistake that he made in his life." Herb's marriage had failed and, after having eight children, Ruth's parents had separated.

It was a very sad day and I felt sick, knowing I had come between a father and daughter. Herb had scratched my truck but, really, what was the truck worth? Over the following day, I wrote one of the hardest letters of my life and apologized to Herb, asking him to come back and stay with us. He did come back to visit, often turning up on our doorstep unexpectedly. Visits were much sweeter after this incident. Herb taught me a lot about the importance of people and I had earned respect through asking for his forgiveness.

Your in-laws

→ *They are your partner's family and honouring them will go a long way.*

→ *Always remember that these are very important people to your husband/wife.*

→ *Try to get to know them.*

→ *Don't make too many personal jokes at their expense.*

Ruth would sometimes stay up at night to study the scriptures while I, tired from hard manual work, went to sleep. All was good until one morning Ruth bravely told me that, while I slept the previous night, God had baptised her in the Holy Spirit and that she had begun to speak in 'other tongues.'

That morning, as I walked away to my farm shed to do my day's work, I wondered, 'While I slept last night this Holy Spirit actually came into my house.' I had stopped Ruth from going to one of these Spirit churches, but could not stop the Holy Spirit from coming into my house. I felt a little like how Adam must have felt – that he should have been with Eve when she ate of the forbidden fruit – but one look at Ruth and I knew this was good and not bad. It felt as though I had been cornered. I considered, 'How can I get this Holy Spirit without looking silly and admitting that I have been wrong all these years?'

Around this time my pastor had asked me to disciple Ian, a school teacher friend of mine. He had been away visiting relatives and came to see me one Monday afternoon. I was walking across the paddock, carrying two ten metre irrigation pipes on each shoulder, when Ian strolled over to me with a huge grin on his face. He excitedly told me that he had gone the previous day to Bundaberg Christian Outreach Centre where some guy called Geoff had prayed for him. Passionately, Ian related how he had fallen under the power of God with liquid love flowing over him. He said that when he came to, he was on the floor with his head under a chair. I could not believe the stuff Ian was telling me. Whatever had happened to my mate? Sensibly, I replied, "Ian, you must have needed it, but this is not for me."

How to disciple someone

→ Remember that discipleship involves relationship.

→ Get into their world, and genuinely care for the well being of the person.

→ Don't consider it a job.

→ Understand that their personality could be very different to yours.

→ Value their time.

→ Be prepared with the scriptures that you will share.

→ Don't argue.

→ Never share the grievances you may have about your church.

→ Be an example.

→ Remember, you don't have to tell the disciple everything you know.

→ Be inspirational about your faith in God.

→ Make the discipleship fun.

It had been seventeen years since my first encounter with the Holy Spirit when sneaking up on Grandad. Unknown to me, God's appointment with me was drawing near. While on my tractor ploughing late one night and feeling ever so empty, I called out to God from the depths of my heart. "If You're up there, please show me what life is about!"

Two weeks later Ruth and I drove away for a short break. By then Christian Outreach Centre churches were springing up in many nearby cities. That morning I decided that it was time to check out the church in Maryborough to see whether those people were still just as happy as they had been seven years before. Instantly I felt at home as I walked in and, at the conclusion of that meeting, I asked the pastor to pray for me to receive the baptism in the Holy Spirit. The living God and I had a fresh encounter that day. This new experience came slowly at first, but throughout the next day His presence flooded my whole being. Now these 'other tongues' were coming out of my mouth, as I prayed and worshipped God.

Awakened from within, I remembered the touch that had affected me all those years before, as I had gone to jump on Grandad. I felt like God had been calling me all those years and I had been ignoring Him.

Melonie, our oldest daughter had been born with a severe allergy to dairy products where even one drop of milk in a bowl of porridge would cause vomiting and severe blisters.

The prospect of her not having milk, cheese or ice cream for her life caused Ruth and I much distress. Reaching out for God to touch our daughter, Ruth and I drove four hours to a healing meeting at Brisbane Christian Outreach Centre.

Arriving early I explained the situation to Pastor Clark Taylor, but he was rather gruff and hastily said for us to bring up our daughter at the end of the meeting. The fact that we had driven so far did not seem appreciated and was quite a shock that irritated me through the meeting. When the time came for prayer, I held Melonie in my arms, hoping Clark would remember me and say a good prayer, but to my disappointment he only patted her on the head and moved on to the next person.

"Mummy, can I have some cheese?" Melonie asked the next day. Ruth and I made eye contact that told a story. Will we try? A little bit, maybe? Yes, we would! There were no reactions to the cheese or any dairy products. God had indeed done a miracle through the pat of Clark's hand, and Ruth and I would soon be selling all in search of the power that was in that pat!

The value of being baptised in the Holy Spirit

→ You become God-conscious rather than self-conscious.

→ A desire to serve God becomes foremost in your life and dreams are stirred to do great things with Him.

→ Your experience with Christ results in victory that is relevant to all of life's circumstances.

→ Your heavenly language of speaking in 'other tongues' releases within your spirit the power and ability to pray far beyond your natural understanding.

→ Boldness comes as you learn to know God and the power of His presence.

→ Your desire is stirred to read the Bible, hear from God and obey Him.

→ The gifts of the Holy Spirit flow much more freely through the believer who has been baptised in the Holy Spirit.

→ You desire and sense the power within you to reach people who don't yet know Christ.

"But you shall receive power when the Holy Spirit has come upon you; and you shall be witnesses to Me..."

(Acts 1:8)

5 *Frozen Fruit Salad*

IIIIIIIIIIIIIIIIIIIIIIIIIIIIIIIIIIIIIIIIIIIIIIIIIIIIIIIIIIIIIIIIIIIIIIIIIIIIIIIIIIIIIIIIIIIIIIIIIIIIIIIIIIIIIIIIIIIIIIIIIIIIII

How could I have missed so much for so long? I would spend weeks ploughing every day and dreaming of making those stacks of money that a kangaroo couldn't jump over, but now I was also praying most of the day with joy and a song in my heart.

On the farm we grew and rotated crops, one of which was rock melons (cantaloupes) which I farmed in partnership with my brother, Tommy. We had grown this crop for several years and had begun to make a lot of profit by producing the melons early, when no one else had them on the market.

In October 1983 the crop was exceptional and the market was very strong. As we walked through the paddock we found the first ripe fruit and knew we would be flooding the markets within weeks. Oh! What a feeling! With light hearted chuckling we could almost feel the money tingling in our pockets, as we made our way back to our house. But I noticed an unusual greenish colour in the storm clouds that were brewing in the late afternoon sky. Over the years I had seen those clouds before. 'But surely not this time,' I thought. 'Surely, not now!'

Within hours I heard the most dreaded sound to any fruit grower – the loud, crashing noise of hail pounding on our roof. Ruth and I looked out of the window to see hail as large as golf balls bouncing on the lawn. We knew the inevitable, that the crops would certainly be ruined. After the storm passed, my quick inspection revealed that our precious, beautiful rock melons had become like frozen fruit salad with lumps of ice going right through the fruit. I found three melons that had been hit by one hailstone. It was as though someone had been shooting at our fruit from the heavens and, whoever it was, he was a good shot! Devastation was everywhere and, even worse, the neighbours who were not churchgoers did not get any damage!

I had been praying for hours every day and now, where was God? I was confused. This didn't happen before I prayed and sought God. Why now?

That night my heart was so very heavy and the feeling of resentment was so close. What had caused this disaster? Was it the devil or was it God? Our crop and, therefore, our money were lost within a few minutes. What would we do for income until we raised the next crop?

My mother had told me about an uncle of mine who had once put his fist up and cursed God when things had not gone well. I was worried I might find myself doing such a thing, if I did not very quickly put my heart right. Closing the door of our spare bedroom, I fell on my knees. There were many questions but no answers.

My intent was to try to find God. Somehow, in the midst of my confusion, I remembered Romans 8:28, *"All things work together for good to those who love God, to those who are the called according to His purpose."*

Praying was not easy with such a huge weight on my heart. I wanted to tell God I still loved Him, but it was just so painful and difficult. After several attempts, my words stumbled out, "I don't know why this happened tonight, but, but I will... will still love You, and somehow I know that You will work it out for good." It seemed as though a stone got rolled away from my heart and that crushing weight that

I had previously felt had lifted. I told God I still loved Him, no matter what!

Later that night, as Ruth and I lay in bed, there was awkward sadness as we wondered about our future finances and practical needs of the next year.

In the stillness of that night, a voice so strong spoke to my heart – a voice that I had never heard before. "Ashley, you have always believed in Me. Why haven't you taken Me seriously? My relationship with you is the most important thing in your life. You have always wanted fruit. If you follow Me, you will have fruit for eternity!"

I was not a fisherman like Peter or John, so Jesus did not say to me, "Come follow Me and you will become a fisher of men." Rather, I was a fruit grower. I was shocked and surprised. Jesus knew all about me and my dreams of growing and producing fruit. "Fruit for eternity?" My God had spoken – to me!

How to hear from God

→ Expect that God wants to speak to you.

→ Still your mind and emotions in His presence.

→ Don't have preconceived ideas as to what He will say.

→ Remember, what God says to you will never conflict with biblical truths.

    "My sheep hear My voice and I know them, and they follow Me."   (John 10:27)

That night the whole focus of my life changed. Although I don't believe all hailstorms are specific 'acts of God', the next morning, as we surveyed the damage, I knew that God had called me to preach the gospel and produce fruit for eternity in the lives of people. I knew we could have continued to run the farm and in a few years would have been on the front foot again. However, a higher call and purpose for our lives was unfolding.

Ruth and I sought advice from the pastor who had prayed for me for the baptism in the Holy Spirit. After we related our hailstone story and about the subsequent voice from God, he said, "If you still feel this way in a month, put your farm on the market and see what happens." Initially I was so surprised that he suggested only a month, but actually that month seemed to take years because the calling grew stronger, day by day. I continue to thank God for this minister who could recognise the calling of God upon our lives.

Recognising your call to ministry

→ However it comes, listen for God's voice calling you.

→ Seek the spiritual counsel of those you respect.

→ Ensure that you are, and remain, under the sound biblical covering of mature Christian leaders.

→ The call to ministry is not so much about us, but rather about helping other people.

I was just a farmer from the bush of Australia who God was calling for His work, and it meant so much to know someone understood what was happening. At that time, the vision for nations had not even entered my mind. I simply carried just a wild passion to follow Jesus and to see eternal, lasting fruit.

One particular night I went out on my tractor to plough, but for some reason I started to preach out loud. In my imagination I saw a crowd of people before me. Becoming so passionate in the preaching, I began to shout the message and asked people to raise their hands, if they wanted to receive God's gift of salvation. I imagined that the tractor muffler was a hand that had responded and was raised, and then I shouted, "I see that hand! Is there another?" In the spirit I then saw many hands being raised. I shouted even louder and more passionately, "Yes, I see that hand also. Come to Jesus!"

That next morning I told Ruth, "If I ever preach to people like I did on the tractor last night, I know people will get saved." The dreams of ministry had begun.

Where could we go to be trained? Pop's friend, Kevin Dales, was now pastoring a Christian Outreach Centre church in North Queensland. One morning I was working in the far paddock and noticed our truck being driven very quickly up the farm track. It was Ruth, pregnant with our second child. She parked the car and hurried towards me. "Kevin has just rung and has offered to personally train us." "Really?" I responded excitedly. It was as though a dream had come true and God had opened the way.

The farm sold quickly. We held an auction to sell the farm machinery and almost everything in our house, including our new slate-top pool table. I felt like Peter and John as they left their fishing boats and nets to obey the call to follow Jesus.

Before leaving we visited Ruth's brother who God had certainly used to bring me into the things of God's Spirit. As we sat together to chat, he asked, "How many men are there that you know of who move in signs and wonders?" I thought for a moment and responded, "Oral Roberts, T.L. Osborn, Clark Taylor," and my current knowledge was depleted. "How many preachers are there in the world?" "Maybe a few hundred thousand," I uttered. "Then, how and why do you think that you will be one of those few who move in miracles?" my brother-in-law quizzed.

It was a good question. I know now that there are many more, but at that time my knowledge of preachers was very limited. Actually, I had not even thought about the odds, because I simply had a dream to preach the gospel. At that moment a strange thing happened. It was as though I was listening to a human voice with one ear and with the other ear I heard God speak, "If you seek Me, you shall find Me." That day, I chose to listen to God above the voice of man. The journey of following Jesus was so exciting. It felt like I had become one of His disciples!

Ruth and I, with our two young daughters, Melonie and Amy, moved 1,500 kilometres to Innisfail, North Queensland. No promised pay or job, but rather a chance to be trained to fulfil the call of God. Our hearts were on fire!

Being trained

→ People are all different with numerous experiences and backgrounds. Never compare your progress with that of another.

→ Some people need emotional healing and character development for their weak areas to become strong (e.g., their ability to trust may be eroded, or family breakdown may have left relational areas that need to be strengthened).

→ Do your homework and study the scriptures for yourself. Your life must be built in personal study of the Bible and not just via your teacher.

→ Your trainer/s will not be perfect, but remember they probably know a lot more about Christian life and leadership than you know.

→ Have a teachable attitude and be willing to be corrected.

→ Decide not to run when the training gets a little difficult.

→ Ask many questions. People who ask questions usually get them answered.

→ Listen more to the people who are training you than to praise from your peers.

→ *Become involved in church life by attending prayer and church meetings regularly. Make good friends at church who you can pray with. It is often said that Christianity is caught as much as it is taught.*

→ *If you want to keep on developing in leadership, have the attitude that we never cease being trained.*

→ *People are called to many different areas of ministry, each with different responsibilities. Greater responsibility will require longer and more intensive training.*

6 The Big, Black Lounge Chair

They call it 'God's Own Country.' The roadside sign as you drive into Innisfail says it all, 'Green like you've never seen.' Lush tropical rainforests, supported by the highest rainfall in Australia, and the continual humidity of a hot house keeps everything alive and growing. There is the annual Golden Gumboot competition for the highest rainfall, but it is always between the three rainfall greats of North Queensland: Tully, Innisfail and Babinda.

Rain is usually in the vicinity of six metres per year and the spiders, cockroaches, mosquitoes, snakes and cane toads are of antediluvian dimensions. On the edge of the rainforests the cassowary, a large flightless bird, is often seen. This strange, flightless bird has a large crest on its head and can attack if annoyed, as our cat one day discovered. Rising sharply from the coastal plain is the large Bellenden Kerr Range and, if it is not raining, the stately, highest mountain in Queensland can be seen, Mount Bartle Frere.

My Grandad, Samuel Dales, had pioneered the Assemblies of God church in this very town some fifty years before. Then three years previous to my arrival, Kevin Dales, my Grandad's nephew and Pop's best friend, had pioneered the Christian Outreach Centre church in Innisfail.

Melonie was three and Amy only six weeks old when Ruth and I followed this call to North Queensland. It felt like a great biblical adventure unfolding before us.

We rented a house with a swimming pool in the back yard and accompanying outdoor access bathroom. Here in this bathroom there was already a toilet and shower, but there was just enough room for me to squeeze in a big, black lounge chair. This became my meeting place with the Spirit of God. For many hours every day, that was where I worshipped God, read the scriptures and met with the Lord. It was like having a personal teacher who led and taught me each morning – as though God was indeed waiting for me to just come and meet with Him.

How to read the Bible

→ *Ask the Holy Spirit to illuminate the words and give you understanding.*

→ *Start with the gospel of John.*

→ *Imagine yourself in the story to make it more relevant to your life.*

→ *Read the scriptures in the full context of the overall passage.*

→ *When you read, think quality rather than the quantity.*

This room became so special to me that, many years after we moved to England, I just longed to go back for a look at this room where God had met me, where up to six hours a day He and I communed together. Years later on a return visit, as I peered into the room I half expected to see the black lounge chair still there, but I was surprised when a dog came out yapping at me. The new owners had made it a dog house, but for me it had been my dedicated, personal sanctuary where God met with me.

Ruth had always been very knowledgeable about the scriptures. I was amazed when I first met her and found how much of her Bible she knew and had highlighted in various colours. She had clearly studied a lot more of her Bible than I had of mine. When I asked her what the coloured passages meant, Ruth explained that those were where it meant special things to her.

Because we had sold the farm, I did not need to work for income, so had time to study the Bible. Ruth allowed me the space to spend a lot of time reading and studying the scriptures. 1984-5 was a fast track in learning all things spiritual and my desire for this was unquenchable.

Even before I arrived for training, Pastor Kevin had told me that fasting from food was necessary for me, in order to develop my inner spirit life. He said that every one of his leaders had to do a ten day fast! But Kevin must have read my mind, because he encouraged me with a big chuckle, "Don't worry, Ash, you won't die. Others are fasting while doing hard physical work at the same time." He continued, "Just remember to drink lots of water."

My first fast lasted two or three days and was so difficult. I worked for most of the day to shut out any thought about food. Being brought up on the farm, I had often had steak for breakfast and had never been without a meal in my life. Now all things changed and my heart towards God sought every key that would unlock His power within my life. Vast amounts of fasting, usually lasting between seven and thirty days, became the norm for my life.

How to fast

→ Decide what sort of fast you will do — fast from solids or from desserts? If only fluids, what sort of fluids (e.g., water only or include juices and tea).

→ *It is not a good idea to have much caffeine during fasting, because you will already sleep less.*

→ *Your marriage partner needs also to understand what sort of fast you will do – will it be a fast of no television and/or no sexual intercourse? Best talk about these things!*

→ *Make sure you enjoy your fast and enjoy seeking God. Decide not to go around with a forlorn face.*

→ *Always drink plenty of liquids.*

→ *The first three days are the hardest. Afterwards, hunger will leave you and you can get down to enjoying a good fast.*

→ *If on a 'fluids only' fast, remember that you could have a run of diarrhoea on about the 8th day!*

→ *When coming off a long fast, avoid all solids for the first day and then chew your food well. Steer clear of big T-bone steaks on the first day after coming off your fast!*

"Is this not the fast that I have chosen: to loose the bonds of wickedness, to undo the heavy burdens, to let the oppressed go free, and that you break every yoke?"

(Isaiah 58:6)

Once when I was fasting, I went to visit my mother who was so concerned at my weight loss that she made a mango smoothie in the blender, kindly encouraging that Jesus wouldn't mind. The more I fasted, the more I wanted to fast. It seemed to unlock something deep within me. It was a craving inside my spirit for heaven to be manifested. I understood what Jesus meant:

"I have food to eat of which you do not know."

(John 4:32)

"Pursue love and desire spiritual gifts."

(1 Corinthians 14:1)

Consumed with a passion to hear from God and to move in the gifts of the Holy Spirit, I prayed earnestly that He would help me understand these spiritual gifts. Many people told me how they had received words of knowledge from God, receiving a pain or tingling feeling in a part of their body, or had a picture come to mind. I was confused about what to expect. I realised that I had to personally hear that still small voice and learn how God would communicate with me.

One day, sitting in my big chair, I asked God about who would be in the coming night's meeting. With my eyes closed, in my imagination I quickly saw a belt buckle with a bull's head on it. It disappeared from my imagination in a second, but I wondered about it and quietly asked God what it meant and who this person could be. I felt strongly within me that the belt buckle belonged to a person with one arm considerably weaker than the other. I wondered, could this be from God? I told Ruth what I had felt.

In the meeting later that night I forgot to give that word of knowledge and, after most people had left, Ruth said, "There is a man here who has a bull's head on his belt buckle." I was so excited and rushed to talk to him, enquiring after his arms. He said, "I broke this arm many years ago and it never regained its strength." I was so happy, not that his arm had not healed, but that I had learnt to hear from God.

After one meeting, a well-meaning friend approached me thoughtfully. Lowering his voice, he commented, "Ashley, I've noticed how accurate you are moving in words of knowledge. I wonder if you've noticed you are more accurate than Kevin these days." I was startled, and in the coming weeks began to notice in myself some superior and prideful feelings. Realising that these feelings had the potential to bring division between my trainer Kevin and me, I decided to put them out of my mind once and for all. Being trained was more important than feeding my ego.

One Sunday Kevin was away and I was asked to preach in his place. This was a rare and exciting opportunity, and I gave it everything. After the service a number of people exclaimed to me how good it was and how much they had enjoyed it. Feeling flushed with success, I wondered briefly why Kevin's wife, Bev, had not given the same compliment. She would surely let Kevin know how well I had done.

On Monday afternoon Kevin returned and phoned for a chat. "Your message didn't hit the mark," he said. My heart sank, and I couldn't wait for the conversation to end. Feeling downcast and annoyed with Kevin, I decided to pray and thereby lift my spirit. "Perth – I am calling you to Perth to plant a church." I seemed to hear a voice within me. Geographically, Perth is one of Australia's farthest cities from Innisfail. I was very excited at this word from God, and came bouncing out of my prayer room to let Ruth know. "God has just spoken to me and we are going to Perth to plant a church." Ruth went quiet and didn't seem as excited. My wise wife has reminded me many times over the years that she knew I had a bad attitude, so she decided to pray about it rather than confront me.

The next morning I was eager to speak to Kevin. "God's calling us to plant a church in Perth," I said confidently. "He hasn't said anything to me," Kevin said bluntly. "Don't worry, He will," I assured him.

As it would take several months to get everything organised for the move to Perth, I now had some spare time. Over the next few weeks I began to feel rather distant from the church, certainly from Kevin and, finally, even from God. What had happened? I was now in no state to plant a church in Perth. Deciding to forget Perth, I amazingly felt at peace with everything and everyone, including Kevin and God! I later realised that my pride had led me to take offence at Kevin's words and that the voice I heard was not

God's. If I had insisted on leaving for Perth, it could have had disastrous and serious consequences for the call of God on my life. Through this situation I came to appreciate my spiritual covering and the importance of letting go of offences.

Overcoming Offences

→ Recognise that offences will come. *"It is impossible that no offences should come, but woe to him through whom they do come!" (Luke 17:1)*

→ A good test to determine whether you are offended: Do you keep thinking about what happened and, when you do, do you feel angry?

→ Recognise that it is sin to take an offence into your heart. To carry an offence breeds unforgiveness.

→ Realise that nurturing this offence will cost you in many ways – in relationships, your joy and your blessing from God.

→ Don't let your mind dwell on justifying yourself.

→ Most times it doesn't matter so much who was right and who was wrong about the issue, but it does matter who takes a bad attitude.

→ Hard as it is, pray blessing on the person who offended you and, if possible, do something good to that person.

→ Come to God in prayer, ask Him to forgive you for taking in the offence and ask for more of His grace. Very seldom does the offence leave immediately. Keep bringing the situation before God until you feel the release of forgiveness in your heart.

→ Never make major decisions because you are offended.

→ Recognise that people have been hurt much more than you and didn't take offence, so it is possible for you to conquer this too!

After a few months of being in training at Innisfail, I started to experience conviction over some issues during my farming years. This began to disturb me so much that, every time I tried to worship, a troubling thought would return. At first, I thought it was a harassing demon and kept telling this 'demon' to leave me alone, so that I could worship God. However, I soon discovered that it really was the Spirit of God urging me to put things right. In the year prior to my baptism in the Holy Spirit, a fuel company had filled my large diesel tank, but they forgot to send a bill. I had thought at the time that it was a blessing. God seemed to really care about this and I could not find the same peace until I yielded. I worked out how much I should have paid, added interest onto it and sent the cheque away. The company wrote back, thanking me and wishing me well in my new career.

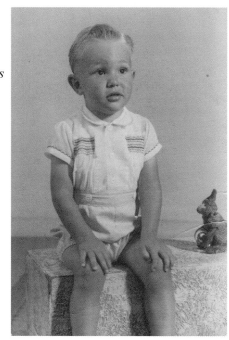

Ashley 2 years

Schmierer children ready for Sunday School: Kerry, Marcia, Pam, Ashley, Russell (Tommy), Lyn (inset)

Ashley's first day of High School

Ashley with his p...
calf, Gyps...

At summit of Ayers Rock, central Australia – Ashley (15 years) paid for this holiday by catching mice

Ashley's parents,
Austin and Joan
Schmierer on their
wedding day,
31st December 1949

Mother Joan with her
fourth child and first
son, Ashley

Ashley with his Grandparents, Samuel and Lily Dale

The man from Gayndah, meaning 'Place of Thunder,' the oldest town in Queensland, Australia

Ashley with his Grandmother, Miriam Schmierer, who lived to be the oldest person in Australia

Farming days

*Ashley, snake killer,
with daughter Melonie*

*shley's farm Mt Debatable,
ayndah, Australia, including
e citrus orchard he established*

Ashley barking trees for building new cattle yards

Beekeeper Ashley

Genuine Clearing Sale

A/c Mr and Mrs A Schmierer who have disposed of their property 'Mt Debatable'

Old Mundubbera Road, 3½ miles from Gayndah

Saturday, April 28 — 10 a.m. sharp

Machinery: Morris 13' chisel plough, trashworker

Clearing Sale advertisement, 1984 – selling all to go and preach the gospel

Ashley and Ruth with the citrus orchard

*Ashley and Ruth –
Wedding Day
17th December 1977*

*Friends in life, partners in
ministry, and diving buddies*

Ashley and Ruth, Melonie and Amy Schmierer, about
to leave Australia for a new life in the UK, 1993

Melonie – Masters,
Cambridge, 2007

Amy – Bar Exams,
London, 2007

7 *A Father in the Gospel*

IIIIIIIIIIIIIIIIIIIIIIIIIIIIIIIIIIIIIIIIIIIIIIIIIIIIIIIIIIIIIIIIIIIIIIIIIIIIIIIIIIIIIIIIIIIIIIIIIIIIIIIIIIIIIIIIIIIIIIIIIIIIIIIIIIII

The lessons came quickly and within a few weeks Kevin sat me down for a fatherly chat. His words shocked me as he said, "Ash, you must trust me with your life." I just smiled but thought, 'No way! I will trust Jesus.' Later when I got home, I told Ruth that Kevin wanted me to trust him with my life. Feeling extremely defensive, I complained, "Sounds like a cult to me."

I struggled with Kevin's words, mainly because of my strong mind and being totally in charge of my life for so long. After my father's death, it was a matter of toughening my mind to survive the challenges of life. Now Kevin wanted me to trust him! It all sounded strange. If this had not happened, I probably would never have been able to be a good student and to be personally trained. Within days, I wondered what the issue was really about. Of course I needed to trust my pastor and trainer.

We were two tall guys squeezed into a mini. When Kevin and I got out of his car, people said it was like two pocket knives opening up. One day Kevin and I were driving past the Innisfail hospital when he said words that reverberated in my heart for years and have affected my whole ministry life. Kevin simply said, "Ash, desire to be a father. To the Corinthians Paul wrote, 'There are ten thousand instructors and very few fathers.' That was the case two thousand years

ago and it is the same today." As soon as Kevin dropped
me off at my house, I went to my office and looked up
the scripture that he had mentioned. I had never noticed it
before, but from this day on it would become pivotal to my
ministry. I prayed, "Lord, Paul said this two thousand years
ago and Kevin said it today. Please make me one of these, a
father in the gospel."

*"For though you might have ten thousand instructors in
Christ, yet you do not have many fathers; for in Christ
Jesus I have begotten you through the gospel. Therefore, I
urge you to imitate me."*

(1 Corinthians 4:15-17)

In the following months there would be many heartfelt
prayers as I fasted and prayed, crying out to God. Whatever
change it meant in my life, I knew this was something that
God had spoken through Kevin to me.

I continued to pray many times a day, "Lord, make me
a father. Paul said it two thousand years ago and now my
pastor has said it. This must be the biggest need, if it hasn't
been fulfilled in two thousand years of church life."

There was always great excitement when a prophet
came to town. Even people who hadn't been in church
for weeks all of a sudden came, hoping God would speak
through the man of God. "Wait here, God has a special
word for you," the prophet spoke. My heart was racing
– was it going to be a good word? "For God has called
you to be a father to the fatherless and indeed a father
in the gospel..." Wow, these were the very same words
that I had been praying and fasting about for the past six
months. God had heard the cry of my heart. It wasn't
just some idle passion, but God was saying that He had
definitely heard me.

What is a father in the gospel?

→ *He reproduces his Christian life's principles into other people.*

→ *He helps guide another in wisdom and understanding.*

→ *He cares spiritually for others.*

→ *He can discipline in love.*

→ *He walks in maturity.*

→ *He encourages and releases others to do what they also do well.*

→ *The above points also apply to 'mothers' in the gospel.*

One Monday morning, I rolled up at the church to see Kevin, but he was so serious and even depressed. I asked, "What's wrong, mate?" "God was not here yesterday," Kevin muttered. Shocked, I exclaimed, "What! Where was He?" He answered despondently, "Don't know, but He wasn't here and we have got a job to find out why He is not here and where He is." Then Kevin spoke the words that alarmed me most. "If God doesn't come back, I am leaving because I won't pastor a church without God!" I couldn't believe his words! Where would I go? Could I buy my farm back? What would I do? What made me feel really terrible was that I hadn't even noticed that God hadn't turned up. Maybe I was so busy seeing everybody else that I hadn't noticed the most important thing!

Quickly I went home and explained to Ruth that we had a major problem – yesterday God was missing from church and Kevin was going to pack up and leave, if we couldn't find out why He'd left and where He'd gone. Where do you start to look for God?

It wasn't as if we could try an advertisement in the newspaper. 'God gone missing' or maybe 'Anybody seen God? Please contact this phone number.'

I was so relieved on Thursday night when Kevin said that He had found God again and the reason why He had not shown up at church the previous Sunday. He explained that the problem was with the musicians and their attitudes. The musicians had been in contention against each other and God was not pleased, but now they had repented and all was well. Wow, that was such a relief! What good is church without God? This incident had an impact on my future church building across the nations where I would one day travel.

Kevin was driving and I was in the passenger seat. "Ash, I'm proud of you," Kevin encouraged, as he reached over and slapped me on the leg. "Thanks, Kev!" I responded appreciatively as I got out of his car. As I walked away, I thought deeply about what Kevin had said. Later that night in my house, the more I thought of it the happier I became. 'Kev is proud of me! He's happy with me,' I thought. For quite a few minutes I sat in my lounge and slapped my leg, just as Kevin had done in the car, and repeated those words. "Kev's proud of me! Kev's proud of me!"

We knocked on every door in Innisfail and all the surrounding towns, up to thirty miles in every direction. Reaching people became our driving passion. Excitement and commitment to see what God would do next was on everyone's mind.

Every Tuesday night Ruth and I, and other leaders, each with a musician would go north, south and west to the nearby towns of Tully, Millaa Millaa, Ravenshoe, and Babinda. I am sure that, if it was possible, we would have also gone east but then we would have been in the Pacific Ocean.

Late one night, as Ruth and I were returning from the Atherton Tableland, a huge python snake was stretched across the road. Hedged in by dense rainforest, not being able to drive over or around it, I took it by the tail and pulled it sideways like a gate that was being opened. The snake was so sleepy that we left it lying across the road in the shape of the letter L.

One evening I was weary and frustrated of just having normal church and told Ruth that I wouldn't eat again until God came with His power. Twenty-one days later, God's power broke through in such a dramatic way that I had rarely seen – a good cause for another week of fasting, just for more of Him.

Prayer meetings were the centre of this great Innisfail church. Whether in the morning or evening they were always well attended. Chas Gullo, a dental surgeon, came dressed in white and we sometimes joked that Jesus had arrived.

One morning, as Chas and I left after an hour of praying, a peculiar thought passed through my mind, "Hey Chas, wouldn't it be funny if one day we were scattered over the nations preaching the gospel?" Although it seems strange to say, we were 'pregnant' with vision and it seemed like anything was possible, if we dared to believe. With amazing accuracy, those words would come true over the following years. Several of us left the shores of Australia and many others went out from Innisfail to do great things for God.

8 *Big Boots to Fill*

Having mostly grown up with farmers older than me, leading young people was not something that I aspired to or felt comfortable with. However, that was all to change when Kevin asked Ruth and me to take on pastoring the youth of the Innisfail church. "I'll think about it," I said reluctantly, hoping that it would never happen. Actually, I felt quite assertive even saying that I would think about it, as usually when Kev spoke we jumped and said, "Yes sir!"

I was only twenty-nine, but it felt like there were several generations between myself and the youth. Actually I did agree to be the youth pastor, but for the next two years it was an education that I forever appreciated. Many rough edges were knocked off of my personality before I could connect with the youth. It was such fun and I would heartily encourage any person aspiring to leadership to master the gift of working with young people. Some of our youth group went on to pastor large churches.

How to be a youth pastor

→ *Enjoy being with young people and have fun with them.*

→ *Don't lecture, but lead them.*

→ *Be passionate and excited about whatever programme is decided.*

70

→ *Give yourself to understanding and reading about youth culture.*

→ *It's good to know of the current bands, songs and movies because young people will certainly be talking about them.*

→ *Don't try to do things like you did when you were a youth.*

→ *Build relationships with the key peer leaders.*

→ *Your messages should be short, creative and full of life.*

→ *Keep an overseeing eye on the godliness aspect of your youth. Remember that you are responsible for them while they are under your care.*

→ *Create opportunities for worship and God's word. Give space for the Holy Spirit to do His work in their hearts. Regularly offer to pray for them.*

→ *Keep the vision to reach lost people before them.*

→ *Among them are your future church leaders, so be inspirational and regularly address the call of God to their lives.*

→ *In their studies and life skills encourage them to do their best. Understand that sometimes they will need to study rather than attend youth meetings.*

→ *Encourage them to always honour their parents and church leaders.*

As the pastor of Innisfail Christian Outreach Centre, a church of three hundred people, Kevin often travelled on mission trips to the Solomon Islands and other South Pacific nations. In his absence he sometimes asked me to hold the fort and oversee the church. These occasions were my first experiences of pastoral responsibility. I felt eager to impress him and hoped no big issues would arrive while he was away.

One such week, two elderly ladies of the church were taken in to the local hospital. As the temporary pastor, I paid them each a visit and reverently prayed over them, but their health rapidly declined. Anxiously, I gathered the other church leaders in the hospital wards to anoint the women with oil, whilst passionately quoting and praying every suitable scripture I could think of, such as James 5:14-15. I had never anointed anyone with oil before, but the situation seemed so serious that I decided to try everything! One dear woman whispered, "Jesus, Jesus," as life ebbed from her body. Then, ninety minutes later the second woman passed away. Despite our fervent efforts, both women had died!

Within days I stood before the coffin of one of the women, having never conducted a funeral before and feeling intimidated by the gathering crowds. 'Neither Kevin nor Jesus told me anything about conducting funerals,' I thought. I had envisioned healings, miracles and masses of people turning to Christ. However, the funeral progressed smoothly and seven people committed their lives to Christ during the service. I wondered if my calling in life was perhaps to conduct funerals. Kevin returned a few days later, and chuckled, "I had to come back and look after my church, otherwise there wouldn't be any people left in it."

Not all people I anointed with oil died!

How to conduct a funeral

→ Visit the closest relative of the deceased in their home.

→ Feel the pain and loss of the family.

→ Connect and pray with the closest of kin.

→ Remember that funerals are when people feel the most open to eternal things.

→ Don't quote Christian promises if the person was not a believer, but rather encourage others to faith in God.

→ *Remember, God comforts the broken hearted and the grieving.*

→ *Be reverent and definitely don't be a judgemental religious zealot.*

In 1987, Kevin called me into his office and told me that he and his wife, Bev, would be leaving the church in Innisfail to take up other responsibilities in Christian Outreach Centre. I was aghast – what would the church do without Kevin? He informed me that Ruth and I would be asked to become the senior pastors of the Innisfail Christian Outreach Centre. I felt privileged, scared and honoured all at once, as I considered the responsibility and the very big boots I needed to fill. Although I had wanted to pastor a church eventually, I had envisaged founding one myself. Innisfail was known as one of the most successful churches in Christian Outreach Centre and, if I made an utter mess of pastoring, it would be very obvious! In addition, Kevin was the founding pastor of the church and was dearly loved by the people, many of whom he had brought to faith in Christ.

A few weeks later Kevin announced to the church that he would soon leave and that I would take his place. Before church that Sunday morning, he and I met in his office. "Ash, today I give you the title of pastor of this church. The title is respected, but you must earn and keep the respect of everyone in this church or they will one day leave." His words followed me from the room. We walked out before the people now gathering in their seats, who had no idea what was about to be announced.

Most people looked shocked, some started to weep, while others clapped and cheered. It was a strange sensation to watch the response. Are they weeping because they don't want me? Are they clapping because Kevin is going?

How to take over leading a church from another pastor

→ Honour the previous pastor.

→ Don't change the church's vision too quickly.

→ Don't demand loyalty or trust towards you – you haven't yet earned it.

→ Love the people who are struggling to receive you and be there for them when a crisis arises.

→ Give people a long time to get to know you in a different light to how they related to you previously.

→ If possible, occasionally get the previous pastor back to preach.

→ Be confident and humble that God has called you to now lead His church.

For several weeks following Kevin and Bev's farewell party, I breathed sighs of relief as everything seemed to be working well. However, this was the calm before the storm. At the monthly leaders' meeting I was surprised at the slackness of punctuality, as department leaders drifted in much later than I had ever seen before. They certainly hadn't done this under Kevin's leadership! Somewhat agitated, I spoke sternly, "If you continue to arrive at meetings late like this, there is going to be a change of some faces on the leadership team." Watching their faces and body language, I perceived that my words were not well received and that I had gone too far. Over the next week I did a good amount of damage limitation. I realised that people had to see and feel the warm, soft-hearted pastor and not the authoritarian man I had been at the meeting. Kevin's parting warning to win the respect of the people would thereafter guide how I lived the next few years.

9 Demon-Possessed Deacon

On my arrival at Innisfail I was met with amazing stories of missionary trips which some of the local church people had been involved in. These were led by Pastors Kevin and Bev Dales who sent mission teams regularly to the Solomon Islands and other South Pacific island nations.

Demons are cast out, the deaf hear and the blind see! These were the reports of those who had been on mission trips. I did not know much about these South Pacific island nations, but it wasn't long before I was looking at a map and booking my first flight to Honiara, capital of the Solomon Islands.

This was serious business and there was a great deal of prayer and fasting before the team departed. By now, prayer and fasting had become a way of life because it was an essential part of leadership in the Innisfail church.

The Solomon Islands are an archipelago of thousands of tropical islands, many of which are small and uninhabited and most with dense rainforests. On those few hundred that are inhabited, most of these South Pacific Islanders are of the Melanesian group, ranging from very dark skin to lighter brown with hair types from tight, black, fuzzy to even blond and wavy. Their particularly slow walk is characterised by their shoes or flip flops dragging on the ground between every stride, giving the immediate impression that the people's legs must be unusually heavy and that life is really slow here. An Islander man once said to me that he didn't like working because it took his mind off Jesus!

These islands were named by a Spanish explorer, Alvaro de Mendana de Neira, who visited in 1568. He found some gold at the mouth of the Mataniko River and erroneously thought that this could be one of the locations in which King Solomon obtained gold for the building of his temple in Jerusalem. Mendana then named the islands after King Solomon – The Solomon Islands. They are also known as the 'Happy Isles.'

There are a few towns on some of the larger, more populated islands but, apart from that, the palm leafed huts of today are similar to those dwelt in by the people of the 'Happy Isles' long before the British colonial rule which ended peacefully in 1977. There is the distinct impression in the remote areas that, hundreds of years from now, life will continue on here without the pressures of diaries and time schedules.

The vast majority of Island people live in villages ranging from 50 to over 1,500 inhabitants and around them are fertile gardens which are enclosed tightly by the rainforests. Some huts have a corrugated iron roof and sometimes a generator can be heard purring away in the distance.

On the island of Guadalcanal, the capital of the Solomon Islands is Honiara which mixes a city with island life. Along the pot-holed, traffic-clogged road is a constant stream of people walking slowly day or night in either direction, while others rest or stand under trees. They all seem to be going somewhere but I never could quite tell where.

How to prepare for a mission trip

→ Pray together, preparing the hearts of team members, so that the whole team is prepared for God to use them and to see miracles on the mission field.

→ Forge friendships by having team meetings prior to departure.

→ Learn which gifts your team members have, and prepare to use each to the maximum.

→ Have practice preaching and testimony sessions. Any practice in working with an interpreter will prove invaluable.

→ Investigate in advance whether you will need vaccinations or to take tablets (e.g., for malaria). Some vaccinations may need several appointments over several weeks.

→ Ensure that each member has travel/medical insurance for the country to which they are travelling.

→ Arrange in advance with your contact person if you will need an interpreter, and check that a good one is available.

→ Recognise that, because of culture and communication problems in some countries, it may be difficult to finalise some details.

→ Educate team members about honouring local church leaders and being sensitive concerning cultural differences.

In the Solomon Islands there are not many western delicacies for those who have a sweet tooth, so on arriving on the outskirts of Honiara, there is often a visit to the hot bread shop where the cream buns are about the best in the city. Otherwise, in the villages your culinary options are limited to taro, sweet potato, slippery cabbage and rice. For the next meal it is rice, slippery cabbage, taro and sweet potato, with the possibility of canned bully beef once a week. Slippery cabbage reminded me of what I would imagine boiled lawn clippings could be like.

It doesn't take long to notice the characteristic red teeth of these Island people and, after this, you see the red patches on the ground. Chewing betel nuts from the Areca Palm, mixed with lime, is the local, cheap drug. The remains of the betel nut are then spat on the ground. It's best to wear shoes!

Those familiar with this region's history are aware of one of the fiercest battles of World War II which took place in 1942, known as the Battle of Guadalcanal. Looking out to sea from Honiara, it might appear tranquil with its dark blue sea, other large islands on the horizon and an occasional Islander fishing from a dugout canoe. This is Iron Bottom Sound and its name bears witness to the huge numbers of ships, planes and submarines buried forever in one the deepest trenches of the Pacific Ocean. They say the sea was red with blood at that dreadful time in history. The might of the American Military was thrown at the Japanese Imperial Army who had occupied these islands from the 7th of August 1942 to the 9th of February 1943. A few miles away is Red Beach where the concrete pads still remain from where the Japanese gunners took their positions. Eventually the Americans broke through. I visited one ridge where it is said that in one night 1,000 Japanese lost their lives while they charged to no avail to take the higher ground.

Indeed, these Isles have not always been happy. On the 20th of September 1871 a missionary, John Coleridge Patteson, was murdered on Nukapu Island at the hands of the natives. Natives had killed him as revenge for the abduction of some natives by other white men. I was very appreciative to have been greeted very warmly on my first visits to the Solomon Islands. These were, to me, many happy times in the Happy Isles!

My first missionary trips to the Solomons were in the 1980's and we were told of a great revival that had swept the nation about ten years previously. It had been particularly strong on the larger, most populated island of Malaita and was reportedly like the day of Pentecost. We were told of a prayer meeting in a hut where the wind of God's Spirit had lifted the roof off, and another where there was a roar of a hurricane around the church but the leaves on the trees were not moving. I remember seeing the glint in the eyes of those who had witnessed these amazing events and I became impatient to see the supernatural in a dramatic way. What God had done before, surely He could do again. Stories of miracles were widespread among these spiritual people. I must say both good and evil spirits are very active in the lives of these Island people.

Our first mission took us to our contacts on Malaita. A small plane flight from Honiara and we landed just outside of Auki, the provincial capital. Then into the back of a truck, the first of many. These are the local taxis, packed with produce of all descriptions and masses of Island people hanging on wherever they can. If there is a place to put one foot, there is room for another person. Once in the truck, you notice, amongst the sacks of potatoes, the odd pig or chickens and mothers breast-feeding their babies on the way to your destination.

In the road the potholes have grown so big that, at times, they are as long as the truck and half as deep, and many times filled with water from the wet season.

How to conduct yourself and a team on a mission trip

→ *Every morning gather the team and meet for prayer.*

→ *Endeavour to eat the food that is put before you.*

→ *Drink plenty of good, clean water.*

→ *Do not complain about the living conditions or food.*

→ *Remember, it is your honour to be in that place representing your local church and, more importantly, Jesus Christ.*

→ *Do not look down on or laugh at the local people.*

→ *Be aware that some people may not appreciate you taking photos of them, especially if you don't know them.*

→ *Obey the local leader's direction in any dangerous situation because they know their nation better than you.*

→ *You and your team must keep any inferred promises or offers to do things for people.*

→ *Look out for cultural differences and make your team aware of them, e.g., in one nation that I go to, if a woman falls down under the power of the Holy Spirit and you step over any part of her body, it is viewed the same as violating her sexually. Be aware!*

→ *Always look for something to learn from the people and the places that you go.*

→ *Commit to God your loved ones who are at home. Beware of home sickness and the dangers of thinking too deeply about home.*

How could a nation be so close yet so different to us? The kitchen is an experience that would cause the most serious chain smoker to cough. A palm leafed hut with a dirt floor and some fire surrounded by rocks in the corner is where the woman of the house prepares the meals.

On one occasion, I was having a rest one afternoon in my hut and I heard shouting coming from outside my window. Jumping up, I went out to see a group of men and women chasing a chicken that had run under my hut. Everyone was armed with a stick as they positioned themselves around my hut, while one Islander crawled under to chase out the ill-fated chicken. Out it came with everyone chasing it, whacking it with their sticks until it died, squawking under the blows. More than once my preaching was accompanied by the squeal of a pig having its throat cut nearby. After a few hours the squawks and squeals did not seem to matter, especially when I realised that it was my evening meal.

My first experience of preaching with an interpreter came in the village of Kakarra. With hundreds of people before me and a man alongside me sharing the pulpit, I then launched into my message. It wasn't long and he said, "My turn." Then he went off in their native language and I looked at him wondering what he was saying. He soon stopped, looked at me and said, "Your turn." Where was I? I took off again only to be interrupted with, "My turn" again. The message was definitely not flowing and I felt myself begin to sweat in anxiety. It turned out to be a very short, unconnected message, bewildering me and everyone who heard it! Preaching with an interpreter requires practice!

How to preach with an interpreter

→ Have a little talk with the interpreter first so he/she gets used to your accent.

→ Your interpreter might want to look at your preaching notes so they can get scripture references ready and understand the flow of your message.

→ Stand on one side of the pulpit and have the interpreter stand on the other.

→ Don't show your frustrations with the interpreter, even if they occasionally miss what you say and have to ask again.

→ Speak a full phrase or half a sentence and then pause for the interpretation. Be aware that speaking one word is often not enough because an interpreter needs more words to work with.

→ As soon as they finish speaking, move in quickly to keep the flow of the message.

→ Avoid long illustrations or stories, because they can take a long time to interpret.

→ *Keep focused on your message and don't listen to what the interpreter says.*

→ *Thank the interpreter for ministering with you.*

Like thousands of other villages in the Solomons, Kakarra had dozens of palm leafed huts, as well as the odd one whose residents were able to afford corrugated iron roofing. It is impossible to paint a palm leafed hut, so all huts have a naturally ageing, brown hue. The floor is raised about one metre from the ground and the grass outside is green and freshly mowed. Grass is mowed in a particular fashion by several people in a row, each swinging long machetes that sweep forward and mow the grass before them. Curious eyes peer from the doorway, watching your every move. Happy, smiling children scamper around the village. These children have no difficulty entertaining themselves, and we attributed this to the lack of television! Shaking tough, calloused hands in greeting reveals the hard manual work in the harsh tropical weather for these Island people, particularly so for women.

The Islanders love to have feasts, and women are often seen cooking 'some stacka good fella kai kai' (lots of good food), while men sit around talking and laughing. The church building is the largest and smartest building, positioned in the centre of the village, with open sides allowing free air flow from every direction. This is air conditioning at its best and also allows the whole village to be filled with their distinctive island singing.

In the months prior to our visit, the people had been searching for God to once again pour out His Spirit. Young people were staying in the church building to pray and then sleep, rather than go home with their parents. In the early hours of one morning I awoke to see the light on over in the church building. Through the dark I wandered and could hear soft voices in the room to the side of the stage. Slowly, I opened the door to find about ten children on their knees, praying. A sense of holiness and reverence for God flooded my heart. It was now after one o'clock in the morning. No parents were present, just children about ten to twelve years of age. A young girl whispered, "Jesus, Jesus, Jesus," as tears flooded down her cheeks. They were oblivious to my presence but this experience would stay with me for the rest of my life. Children don't normally stay up to the early hours of the morning, praying. Surely there was a great move of God's Spirit underway.

The next evening in the Kakarra church we would see and hear an amazing miracle. After a song service an Island woman from that church fell to the floor, shaking violently as the pastor tried to calm her. This is not unusual for these Island people, and at first the pastor thought it was a demon.

Beginning slowly, then becoming louder and faster, she began to speak in fluent English, declaring that God had sent these people from a foreign land to bring the word of God to their village. The word from God was to be obeyed and the Spirit was not to be grieved.

The meeting quickly went silent as she spoke and the pastor quickly came to whisper to us that this lady could definitely not speak any English. After she stopped speaking those words from God, she never again could speak English. This indeed was a sign from God and a great miracle for all who were present.

The exciting thing about walking with God on the mission field is that you never know when the major event will happen that will affect the rest of your life and future ministry.

The opportunity came for me to leave the group of Australian people who had come with me and to go up alone to Rouri, a small village north of where we were staying. The rest of our group had meetings to do and now the gospel was needed in another place, so I would go alone for a few days and travel by truck through the jungle to the next village.

Rouri was next to the shore and is a beautiful little place, however there was nothing arranged for the visiting preacher. They showed me my hut and didn't seem bothered as they presented a huge bowl of sweet potato to me. I sat down to eat while one Islander ran through the village and another went by bicycle, shouting in Pigeon English that in an hour the meeting would begin. "Him fella Ashley preachum big fella Jesus!"

This was my opportunity to make a lasting impression on these Island people. After all, they had not seen a missionary for six months and I had the message, 'God's power in the earth today.' The church building was the conventional palm leafed hut with open sides, crushed coral on the floor and, for seating, two short blocks of a log with a wooden plank between them. Within an hour or so about sixty people had assembled. After a short, lifeless song service I delivered my 'power' message. I thought it went well, although afterwards no one wanted prayer. "A sore knee? A back problem? Does anyone want me to pray for you?" No one responded. The villagers just stared at me curiously, as if I were mad. That is even more amazing, because over the coming years I found out everyone has back and knee problems from working in the village gardens! But none that night wanted me to pray for them.

They were smiling as they walked me to my hut where my bed would be, but in my heart I was feeling discouraged. Something had gone wrong and nothing had happened. In my hut there was just a mat but no mattress and it was going to be a long night. I lay down and cried. What had gone wrong? This was not what I had been told happens when you go on a mission trip. "Jesus, where are You? What happened to those stories of revival, of the deaf hearing and the blind seeing?"

Everything was quiet, then a small voice came to my heart. "You preached your message. Tomorrow I want you to preach Mine." I said, "Lord, what is Your message?" He seemed to whisper to my heart, "The love of God." I said, "Lord, I was hoping to see miracles." And I felt the Lord say, "You can have it your way if you like." It took about half a second to realise I had done it my way and now it was to be God's way. Peace came to my heart as I laid my head on the pillow. The bed was normal for these people but not for me, I must say. It was very hard, so I turned like a chicken on a rotisserie to try to ease or spread the pain.

I woke early and made my way to the nearby creek for a quick bath – shorts on, towel over my shoulder and soap in hand. As I reached the water, I glanced over my shoulder to see more than one hundred Island children following me like the Pied Piper. They had obviously not seen a white man have a bath before. Rather self consciously I lathered up and bathed, as rows of children lined the bank, sitting and showing their white teeth while grinning and chuckling at me.

The message was short that morning, as I had not preached on 'The love of God' before. As I announced my subject there were many smiles and an instant "mm" of approval from across the congregation. It caught me by surprise because this had not happened the night before. At the close of the service I asked if people wanted me to pray for them and the whole church came forward.

There was such a beautiful presence of God and I began to pray along the line of people who had assembled in front of me. As my hands reached to touch the man second in the line, he stated growling and groaning. Deciding that this must be a demon, I wondered what to do. "Jesus!" I shouted, and he staggered back and collapsed to the coral floor. I could tell the pastor was quite flustered as he whispered in my ear that the man now being delivered of demons was, in fact, one of his church deacons! Maybe his was not the only church to have demon-possessed deacons, but it certainly had the pastor worried. At the end of the meeting a man blind in one eye came up to me and asked for prayer that he would see. I prayed so simply and then he smiled and said, "I see!" Word of that miracle travelled through the island faster than we could go by truck.

That meeting and the night prior would affect my life and all my future preaching. I had my heart tested and had learnt a lesson. Jesus always has a message and a word to speak, and it is always better if we preach His word rather than ours!

A few days later back in Auki, the provincial capital on Malaita Island, I was praying for a man who had recently had an operation on his stomach. It had not been successful and the doctors could not locate the source of his pain. This problem was not a physical problem but a spiritual one, and they had done a medical operation to no avail. As I reached out my hand to pray for him, to my surprise he was thrown onto the floor as a demon was driven out of him.

Later that night as I lay in my palm leafed hut, through the open window the moonlight was streaming in. Puzzled, I raised my hand, looked at it and wondered, 'Whatever is in this hand? A few years ago this hand was milking cows. Tonight, as I stretched it towards that man, he was thrown on the floor. There is now an invisible power at work. Something really is inside me and in this hand.' As I pondered the events of that night, I decided, 'This is going to be exciting. I want to see more!'

10 *Put Your Hand Over Your Shoulder*

Crusades in football fields were what I had dreamed of for so long and now the opportunity had come for this in the Solomon Islands. A village in southern Malaita invited us to come and do some special meetings with the local Anglican priest as my interpreter.

Once the music started, a crowd quickly formed as villagers emerged inquisitively from their huts. As the local priest was my interpreter, they seemed very interested in this unusual combination, hearing my message in their native language. My short healing and salvation message finished with a call for lives to be committed to Christ. Abruptly my interpreter left my side, came to stand in front of me and eagerly said, "Me first!" At that point hundreds of people moved forward, first with an embarrassing shuffle and then with more assurance and smiles, as all followed the example of the priest.

About six months later I had the opportunity to return to that same place, so I enquired on how the spiritual revival in that village was now going and how the churches had grown. "There has been no difference," came the hesitant reply. In fact, no more were part of the local church and no lives had apparently been permanently impacted by the amazing meeting only six months before.

This result – or lack of result – marked a turning point in my life, causing me to think seriously about the strategy for mission work and of the need for remaining fruit from the ministry that we do. This would have an effect on all the future nations that I would visit and be instrumental in the vision of training national pastors to go out and establish new churches.

As a young pastor full of dreams to do great things for God, I had heard it said many times by Clark Taylor, the founder of Christian Outreach Centre, that in the vision for Australia we needed a man for every town and that we would simply keep on reproducing. Australia was not building more towns or cities, but there would certainly be more of us! These words, together with my experience of the crusade in the football field and subsequent lack of disciples added to that village church, would give me a vision for training future church leaders.

How could this happen in the island nations of the South Pacific? In many places there are no cars or telephones, just villages surrounded by tropical jungle. As we prayed about the vision, it became clear that the best way forward was to establish a ministry training school in a South Pacific island nation where the people could be trained in their own Island culture. We explored options and land was generously made available at Balasuna (Mbalasuna) village near Honiara, Solomon Islands.

We rarely had money in advance for this work in the South Pacific and often had to proceed initially in faith. Dave, a builder from the Innisfail church, organised the plans for building the complex. We sent carpenters to Honiara with instructions to open a bank account to enable us to transfer money when they needed it. You can imagine how extremely relieved and grateful I was when Alan, an Australian businessman, handed us a large cheque which paid for the construction of the whole complex!

Making your vision a reality

→ Clarify the overall objective. What do you want to achieve?

→ Whatever your vision, you will require much perseverance, patience and faith. You must be totally sold on your vision. Where there is a 'God Vision' there is 'God Provision.'

→ List the resources you have – your personal skills and giftings, material resources, working relationships with other people and their abilities.

→ You won't have everything you need. Identify what you need so you can believe God for those necessities.

→ Identify the strategic people who may support the vision.

→ Other people will want to be a part of your vision when their personal contribution is valued.

→ Break your vision down into bite-sized pieces. This makes it more readily accessible for other people to see what they can do and be part of.

→ If your vision is a ministry within the local church, it must involve reaching lost people or strengthening and multiplying disciples.

Who would oversee the Ministry Training School and where would ongoing support come from? There were many questions, but God slowly made His plan clear. Murray and Diana, a couple in the Innisfail church, would go with their young family to become the college principals who would oversee the training of church leaders. Murray and Diana at that time had three young children. The youngest being only weeks old, they left Australia to live in an island village in an unfinished building with no running water. They planned to stay for six months, but continued to serve as principals of the Ministry Training School for eight years, overseeing the training of hundreds of pastors for the South Pacific nations.

These Pacific Islands have some of the most beautiful coral reefs in the world. Viewed from the air, the turquoise colour of coral reefs surrounding the islands has always caused me to appreciate the creativity of God. Many times I hopped from island to island on a small plane, pressing my face to the window to get a clearer look at one of the most beautiful sights on earth. These planes would land on grass strips that often were the length of the tiny islands. When taking off, at one end of the airstrip, the pilot stills the plane with brakes on and the propeller turning furiously, then quickly releases the brake, causing enough momentum to lift off by the end of the runway. I often felt we should all jump a little in our seats as it approached the runway's end, to ensure lift off!

The world under the sea is a realm to be enjoyed and explored. It reminds me of the spiritual unseen world that is all around us but very few people ever see it.

I qualified for my scuba ticket in Australia, and decided to do a wreck dive with Murray in the Solomon Islands. I put on my tank, BCD vest and weights, then turned on the air and followed Murray into the water. Rather confidently we strolled in up to our knees then, slipping on our masks and fins, we descended through the beautiful, crystal clear water.

Sinking down the side of the Bonegi I, a Japanese transport ship, Murray pointed to the huge torpedo hole blasted into the ship's hull. After being hit, the captain had made the decision to ram the stricken ship towards the beach in the hope to save his crew.

As we continued deeper, I noticed with each breath it was harder to draw air from the tank. Now at over twenty metres,

I glanced at my gauge and noticed with alarm that each time I breathed air the gauge flicked to zero.

Something was clearly wrong, but Murray was three or four metres away. Swimming up, I slapped him on the leg and pointed at my air gauge. At the moment he looked, I was exhaling and the gauge was normal. He just gave a big grin, an ok buddy sign and swam off deeper. Descending further, my head began to feel strange as I tried desperately to draw air. Anxiously I thought, 'What is happening? God, where are you?' Immediately, I heard that voice, "Put your hand over your shoulder and turn on the air." What? Surely I wouldn't have forgotten to turn on my air? Quickly I did as the voice had instructed me and, finding the knob of the air tank, turned it. Suddenly I could feel my breathing become easier. My head slowly cleared.

At depth more air is needed. I had only turned the knob a half turn and was okay for the first few metres. One lesson for life is to fully turn on the air and another is to hear God speak. He knows all things and saved my life that day. Murray just laughed as I later explained what had happened.

The ministry training school was now pumping out trained pastors and leaders for many Pacific nations. Often I would take people from our Innisfail church to the Islands, so we could spend some time together and get to know each other. Fred, a plumber, would come with me on one such visit. In our school we regularly had question and answer times for our students and, since Fred was with me this particular time, he would help me out.

"What do I do with a man who comes to my church and he has three wives with children by each wife?" asked a Papua New Guinea student. As I scrambled blindly for something to say, Fred spoke up[1]. He spoke so strongly with great wisdom and compassion, so from that day forward I knew there was a ministry call of God on his life. It surprised me and I wondered, "Where did that come from?" I thought Fred was kind of a rough character and just didn't fit the usual template of a person who you would expect to do great things for God. Fred and his wife, Mary, formerly a Maltese nun, would go on to live as missionaries and plant many churches in Chile, and then in Malta.

In 1991, on a visit to the ministry school, Murray told me he was short of rooms, warning, "Sorry Ash, you will have to share the room with another guy but I just wanna let you know he snores loud." "No way, mate, put me in another room!" I immediately responded but Murray informed me that the only room available had no mosquito screens. I weighed up mosquitoes or snores for one night and, being a light sleeper, mosquitoes were preferable.

About three weeks after returning to Australia, I decided it was time to go away for a few days for some fasting and prayer. After arriving and praying for several hours, my body began to shake. Was it the anointing or not? If this was God coming upon my life in a powerful way, it certainly felt strange. I thought God would surely bring a good sensation but this was not comforting in the slightest. As a few more hours past and the shaking became uncontrollable, I decided that if this was not God I might need help. Slowly I drove back home amidst the increasing shaking, and now cold and hot spells. As I turned into our driveway, I was relieved to

---

1   What Fred said: Titus 1:6-7 Elders are to have one wife. In some cultures, like in Bible times, having more than one wife has been accepted in society for thousands of years. If a man has more than one wife, he can't reject them for this is his commitment to them. If he were to disregard some after being in wedlock, they are vagabonds in the village and can be abused by anyone. This is not God's will. The man should take no more wives and care for the ones he has, but he should not be a spiritual elder of the church.

see that Ruth was home. One look at me and she knew it was serious!

Ruth quickly drove me to the nearby Innisfail hospital and steadied me as I walked through the hospital doorway, now weak while shaking with both hot and cold turns.

I was examined and admitted into hospital, while Ruth dashed home to collect a few spare clothes. Finding out where I had recently travelled, it was easy for the medical staff to diagnose that it was not the anointing but, rather, malaria! During hot spells when my body seemed to be on fire, pulling the sheets back did little to help. Then within minutes a cold shiver came with uncontrollable shaking and such teeth-chattering that my fillings threatened to fall out. Chewing the sheet helped to ease the chattering of my teeth, and every few hours the nurse came in with a big needle, threatening, "Roll over! It's time for another injection!"

I remember thinking, 'Come quickly, Lord Jesus, and take me home.' It's amazing how your thoughts can change as I pondered what heaven would be like, meeting all the Bible characters and the saints who have gone before. For a few moments I dreamt of meeting martyrs, then those who had been thrown to the lions asking me what it was that finally took my life. "A mosquito," I would say. As they would explain the last moments of their life while they were thrown to the lions, they would ask how big the teeth of a mosquito were… To save face I realised I had to survive this and not die!

I know that many precious people die from malaria, but this was not my time. Maybe the lesson to be learnt was to sleep in the room where the guys snored and not choose the mosquitoes next time!

11 *Let's Kill Him*

IIIIIIIIIIIIIIIIIIIIIIIIIIIIIIIIIIIIIIIIIIIIIIIIIIIIIIIIIIIIIIIIIIIIIIIIIIIIIIIIIIIIIIIIIIIIIIIIIIIIIIIIIIIIIIIIIIIIIIIIIIIIIIIIII

The remote islands of Santa Cruz are the furthest south of the Solomon Islands, close to the northern islands of Vanuatu. The Spanish explorer who named these islands, Alvaro de Mendana de Neira, arrived on his second voyage on the 8th of September 1595. Mendana had hoped to establish a settlement here but died of disease a mere six weeks after arriving. He left his wife as governor of this new settlement, but within two weeks she and the remaining Spanish explorers abandoned Santa Cruz. While Mendana was dying, he must have tried to convince his wife to carry on doing the work. However, she didn't catch the vision and soon headed for home. For centuries after this, almost no explorers visited these islands.

By 1989 Christian Outreach Centre had several churches on Santa Cruz and we needed to find future leaders to train in our Ministry School at Balasuna, Honiara.

It seemed a long, two hour flight from Honiara to Santa Cruz with only the blue waters of the Pacific Ocean below the small, twin engine plane. Several years previously, a plane missed its destination, ran out of fuel looking for land and plunged into the ocean. I thought of that ill-fated plane as we flew from Honiara, hoping our pilot was a better navigator.

A woman with our group found that an unlucky Chinese meal the night before was not good preparation for the flight.

Trundling through the air over the Pacific Ocean, the only place to relieve her poor bowels was into a plastic carrier bag, a few feet away from the rest of us, behind the back seat of the small plane. Apart from a little embarrassment and loss of some personal dignity, we arrived safely.

In the village I was shown my room which had no door and, as I unpacked, a man came in and settled down to look at me. I guess he had not seen an Australian unpacking a suitcase before. In the Island culture they share everything in common, whereas Western culture divides up items into personal possessions kept behind shut doors.

Coming out of my hut, I asked my new friend the location of the toilet. He pointed a certain way and said politely, "Men this way; women that way." I ventured along the narrow path through the tropical rainforest, only to come to a beach. The men's toilet was one part of the beach; the women's was also on the beach but just around the corner. There were people fishing from a few canoes about eighty metres out. Sheepishly I looked around and, feeling somewhat embarrassed, I slowly dug a hole in the sand. I scratched something with my hand and to my shock I found that someone had been in the same spot before me! At that moment I discovered an instant cure for biting fingernails and cautiously dug the next hole with my toes.

Essentials to take on a mission trip

→ Bible, notebook and a few pens

→ Diarrhoea tablets

→ If going to a remote village, it's good to take a roll of toilet paper.

→ Take a surplus of any personal medication you may need.

→ If in a country prone to malaria, always take your tablets.

→ *Take some cash in the local currency. In some countries the local currency can only be bought at an exchange point within that country and you may not be able to change it outside the country. Don't assume that an ATM machine will be available.*

→ *Take suitable clothing for the climate, e.g., sunglasses and hat.*

→ *Good walking shoes; band-aids/plasters; not your best clothes. Try to keep luggage to a minimum.*

→ *Take a photocopy of your passport and keep it in a different place.*

→ *For beginners – take a few muesli bars when going really remote.*

→ *Most importantly, take a sense of humour and a lot of grace.*

The next day we crammed into the back of a truck and drove to the other side of the island. After bouncing around for two hours, the truck suddenly stopped and the driver told us he would meet us here in two days at a certain time. Now 9pm and dark, we followed the leader single file through the jungle. An occasional person carried a lantern and suitcases weighed on our shoulders, as we made our way along the track. In most parts we were ankle deep in mud, and the night sky could not be seen because of the thick jungle that met overhead. There was much chatter in Pigeon English and a good bit of laughing, as we trudged along the path. Down a steep descent over rocks that could have been a cliff, and I was told that we were almost there. In single file we wound past village huts and arrived at 11pm to find all the people waiting in the church building for a meeting.

It was rather a short meeting with a group of really appreciative people. Afterwards there was a good meal of sweet potatoes and we headed off to bed at 1:30am. These people don't get many visiting ministries and make the most of those who do visit. Another meeting was scheduled for 7am.

Later that day many were baptised in the sea a few metres from the church. Hundreds gathered on the rocky coral shoreline, singing with a guitar as we baptised people in the water. There was a party atmosphere and a sight to remember forever, as the crowd of onlookers sang their Island songs, so happy for the changed lives of those being baptised.

At the special evening celebration the church was packed and there was a buzz in the air. The place was lit only by a single lantern just above the musicians. The music still had the South Pacific Island beat but was wild and exciting, with the keyboard player and guitarists dancing and leaping into the air as they played. I glanced around to see the smiles of so many thankful people who had taken me into their hearts. One huge man not far from me was once the hardest criminal of the island and had been in prison for murder, but now I watched as he sang without a care in the world.

The power of God was present to touch people and faith was stirred in hearts as I gave the invitation for people to be baptised in the Holy Spirit. Young and old, male and female, about thirty shuffled forward to be prayed for and many received the baptism in the Holy Ghost while standing, sitting or lying on the coral floor of the church building.

Everything seemed to be so peaceful and beautiful, as the Lord by His grace had touched many with His Holy Spirit. As I stepped back into the crowd of church people, someone whispered in my ear, "Persecutors have arrived and they have surrounded the church." At that point I wondered, 'Persecutors? Who are they? I don't recall having met one of them before.'

Then I saw through the fading light at the back of the church a group of men, some wearing bandanas. My heart nearly stopped as I began to comprehend the situation. These guys did not look friendly! There were shouts and a rock flew towards the front of the room. Then a crash – the glass of the only lantern. It was so dark I could not see a thing, while all around were shouts of angry men. A woman cried out and I suspected a rock had hit her, but the church people sat quietly with just a murmur of prayer amongst the angry shouts. Although the commotion lasted perhaps twenty minutes, it felt like hours before a lantern was brought into the meeting and the village chief persuaded the persecutors to leave. Where was our former criminal man to protect us? There he was – in the dim light I could make out his large frame as he sat quietly praying. Women wiped blood from a middle aged Island sister's face. Later we discovered that the man who threw the rock was actually the son of the woman it hit.

The persecutors left and peace returned as the people slowly disappeared into the darkness, making their way back to the huts. I told the pastor that at first light I would leave and make my way back up the cliff and towards the road. His words chilled me. "Pastor, they will be waiting for you along the path. It is not best for you to go alone. It is best for you to have us on each side of you."

After breakfast about twenty of us began our journey back along the winding path we had trudged two nights previously. While we walked single file through the jungle and then past the village huts, I thought about the beautiful baptism service the day before. Immersed in happy thoughts, I suddenly found before me an angry Island man wearing a bandana, shouting at me. My eyes went to the large stick in his hand. Very quickly some of us were surrounded and cut off from the group, as the men circled us. Many of them had rocks in their hands, half crouching and angry as they walked around us. Mostly the talking was in their own native dialect but some spoke in Pigeon English which I was familiar with. I could make out that they wanted a meeting to put us on trial. 'Trial?' I thought. 'What if I am found guilty?'

There were no smiles as my Island friends sought to intervene, pleading to let me go on my way. In my hand was my video camera and I wondered if I should film something. A furious man stormed over to me. He looked mad and was shouting in his language as he came towards me and then looked into my eyes. He pointed at my shoes and shouted in Pigeon English, "A few years ago your ancestors came here and we only left the rubber from their shoes. That was all that we did not eat!" I decided to leave the video camera in its case and abandoned all thoughts of exciting film footage. Solemnly taking stock of the situation, three appalling thoughts occurred in quick succession: (a) this is very serious, (b) this could be it, and (c) I didn't think it was going to end this way.

As I was realising this could become very ugly indeed, someone shouted, "Let's kill him!" The shout came from behind me, then a stinging pain as a rock hit my lower back. Commotion and noise everywhere, a man approached me and whispered, "I am going to get you out of here right now, follow me!" His words startled me into action and I followed him at a brisk pace. There was mayhem everywhere but we didn't look back or stop until we had climbed a steep embankment in the jungle track. There was still a lot of shouting coming from the valley below, and here we took a moment to look and reflect on what had just happened. Some more men from our group caught us up and we continued through the jungle for several hours. I don't know who that Islander was, but it reminds me of the time that Jesus was taken to the edge of a cliff by an angry crowd, but then walked through the crowd because His time was not yet (Luke 4:29-30). I was glad my life was not yet over, and that more than my shoe rubber would make it out of Santa Cruz in one piece.

We walked back along the jungle path through the ankle deep mud to meet the truck, as agreed two days before. Others of our Island friends arrived and told me what had happened after we had left. When I had been hit with the first rock, one of our men ran up to the persecutors, imploring them, "Don't kill him but kill me instead." They threw the rock, hitting him in the head, causing him to lapse into unconsciousness. His wife was in their hut and, hearing the terrible noise, came out to see her husband lying on the ground. She thought he was dead and started to shout, "My husband has been martyred for Jesus!" A few minutes later he became conscious and I always hoped she was not disappointed that he wasn't killed.

What to do when a major crisis happens on a mission trip

→ *Keep calm because there is always a way forward.*

→ *Listen to the senior leaders whom you know in that country and always take their advice. They understand the dangers of that country. If the problem is serious, notify your travel insurers on their emergency helpline.*

→ *Ask for and keep all receipts for costs incurred, as you may be able to reclaim these from travel insurance. In some cases, a police incident number may be required.*

→ *Tell someone else about your problem. Don't suffer in silence or embarrassment.*

→ *Pray and believe God for His hand of intervention.*

It had been an eventful few days but, while we were relaxing that afternoon, the governing Premier of the island asked to see me to ensure I was okay and did not depart with a negative impression of his people. I assured him of our great love for the people of Santa Cruz.

The annual Solomon Islands Ministry School graduation was a unique experience. Students borrowed suits from their relatives and friends, often several sizes larger than they were. With no electricity apart from the college generator it was still essential to have everything ironed and smart. Often their suits would be pressed but no shoes were available. One student walked to the front, awkwardly lifting his feet, as if to say this was the first time in his life that he had worn shoes and they were very heavy.

One year a student came forward looking ever so smart, shook my hand and told me that he was one of the persecutors who had surrounded the Church the previous year. After we left Santa Cruz, he had felt great conviction upon his life and had given his heart to the Lord. He felt called to ministry and where else did he come but to our Ministry Training School! I had no idea of his conversion until he told me at the graduation.

Just as Paul (Saul of Tarsus) was persecuting the Church and was intercepted by the mercy of God, so this man also had that same testimony.

From our Ministry Training School at Balasuna, near Honiara, hundreds of pastors would go out across the Solomon Islands, Vanuatu, Papua New Guinea, Fiji and Tonga to plant new churches in their villages, towns and cities. These men and women would carry the flame of revival for their lands. The Ministry Training School went on to produce many fine men and women of God and it is reported that, over the following years, some have raised the dead.

I have walked past the graves of some of my men, feeling both sad and proud, recalling their eager faces as they were first sent into ministry. The life expectancy in the Islands is low. Some have died from malaria, while others will never have a grave, as their canoes have been lost travelling between islands in the cause of the gospel. Many new leaders have come through and now carry the baton to change their lands, for the dream of revival never dies in the heart of our people in these Happy Isles.

12 *Don't Blame Me*

IIIIIIIIIIIIIIIIIIIIIIIIIIIIIIIIIIIIIIIIIIIIIIIIIIIIIIIIIIIIIIIIIIIIIIIIIIIIIIIIIIIIIIIIIIIIIIIIIIIIIIIIIIIIIIIIIIIIIIIIIIII

Innisfail, on the coast of North Queensland, is often struck by cyclones, including two of Australia's worst in the last hundred years. In 2006 Cyclone Larry unleashed winds of almost 320 km per hour or 200 miles per hour. In the winds of a cyclone, metal road signs can be flattened and loose objects of any description become missiles flying horizontally through the air. After Cyclone Larry a fence paling was found embedded in an electricity pole, driven in by the force of the wind.

During Cyclone Winifred on the 1st of February 1986, we were barricaded in our house, listening to the roaring of the wind. With every gust of wind, we wondered how much more our brick house would take, and what was left for Winifred to unleash. From our windows we saw garden sheds tremble for a few minutes, then explode and fly away like pieces of paper in the wind, perhaps leaving behind a lonely lawnmower on the concrete base. I looked out of the back window of our house, saw the neighbour put his hand up to the window and waved back at him cheerily. Within moments the window and wall that he had tried to hold up collapsed, as he ran away to take cover from the flying debris. Minutes later my neighbour's whole house was demolished and flying away just like the garden sheds. Fortunately the family escaped to safety.

Mortified, I realised I had been waving while they were desperately trying to support the walls of their home!

Dorothea McKellar's poem, 'My Country,' has a special place in many Australian hearts. I learnt it as a child at school and, after moving to the United Kingdom, would think of it often.

I love a sunburnt country,
A land of sweeping plains,
Of ragged mountain ranges,
Of droughts and flooding rains.
I love her far horizons,
I love her jewel-sea,
Her beauty and her terror –
The wide brown land for me! [1]

Australia is a land of extremes with cyclones, floods, bushfires and droughts, but strength has been forged through these natural disasters. The community spirit of small Australian towns flourishes in such adversity, as social barriers are removed and people willingly come to each other's aid.

We used our church bus for outreach meetings into neighbouring towns. One night on the way back from one such outreach, my assistant pastor, Dan, called me from the outskirts of Innisfail, reporting an incident with our bus. I drove my car out to the highway, and there it was. The bus sat stranded like a beached whale across the middle of the Bruce Highway, the main coastal highway of Queensland. The police car's blue flashing lights lit the night sky as people milled around. The police were directing traffic into the cane fields to get around our bus. One set of the back

1 By arrangement with the Licensor, The Estate of Dorothea Mackellar © Curtis Brown (Aust) Pty Ltd

dual wheels was missing and the motor sat on the bitumen road. I will never forget the look on the policeman's face as he walked over to me and asked, "Is this your bus?" At that moment I would have loved to have told a lie, but I was the pastor and many of my people were listening. Awkwardly I stepped forward to take ownership and confessed, "Yes. This is our bus." "Get it off the road!" he responded forcefully.

This bus weighed tonnes, was totally immobile and was blocking the Bruce Highway. I imagined film crews and helicopters flying overhead, then newspaper headlines: 'Church bus loses wheels, blocks highway', 'Church stranded as it loses its wheels' or 'Church leaders can't be found – gone into hiding'!

Our youth pastor, Charlie, stepped forward, "At my business I have a forklift. Do you think that will work?" "Let's give it a go!" Within a short space of time we were positioning the forks under the rear of the bus. The policeman gave us no encouragement, shaking his head with arms folded, but I was praying, "Lord, help me get this thing off the road tonight before the TV crews get here." Inch by inch, the bus was nudged a few feet at a time until finally it sat forlornly at the side of the road. We never found those back wheels which must have hurtled into the tall sugar cane.

My heart and love for people kept growing stronger and a desire to reach people with the love of Christ began to grip my heart. The old shy Ashley who did not relate to people and tried to avoid talking to them seemed to be losing the battle. The continual prayer of my heart would be, "Lord, give me souls, lots of them. I want to preach your word to the multitudes."

Praying often for people to come to God, I cried out passionately to Him. "Lord, please give me many souls, towns, cities and even nations!" I then thought for a moment, 'Oh! Did I say nations? Who am I to talk of nations? I must have become too proud.' I prayed again, "Lord, please forgive me for my pride. I will only ask for ones and twos." But soon my desire overtook my mind again and I started to cry out for nations. I then reasoned, 'It sounded good and I should not repent for asking God for too many people.' Never again did I apologise for asking God for too many souls! At times I would go for walks at night in the park, praying and sometimes lying on the grass, weeping for people and for nations. Never in my wildest dreams could I have imagined that one day God would grant me the privilege of preaching His gospel to so many nations beyond the shores of Australia.

Within me a father's heart was slowly growing and the sense of how to release God's compassion to His people now began to dominate my life.

Alan was a good friend of mine and a leader in the church. He and his wife were most upset about something that was a big issue for them, and had decided to leave the church. Sitting in their home, I started to weep as he adamantly informed me of their decision to leave, even though they had no plan of where to go next. 'Where will they go?' I thought, as I felt great sadness. I loved this couple but it appeared that nothing could be said to turn them around. Most people leave churches because of misunderstandings, and I have seen pastors keen to see the back of people who have become disgruntled. However, misunderstandings can almost always be resolved if a pastor will take time to truly understand and address the source of their discontent.

An hour later a call came through to my office. It was Alan. "Ashley, we can't leave your church. You love us so much. We would never get another pastor who would love us like you do." I felt huge relief at hearing these words, and glad that my love and pastor's heart had so affected these wonderful people.

Then there was Mrs Newman, a grumpy, seventy-nine year old lady who owned a corner store. Although her grandson was the church drummer, she disliked our people, excited from Sunday meetings, and would chase them from her little shop. However, one Sunday night Mrs Newman came into the church and sat near to the front row, just to see her grandson play.

She sat like an immoveable stone and even a passionate altar call for salvation did not move Mrs Newman. Sitting next to her at the close of the meeting, I chatted with her and asked again, but still no response. I pointed to the church door and reasoned, "Mrs Newman, just like people are going through that front door, so Jesus is the only door to heaven." She glared at me stonily. I asked, "Do you think Jesus would let you into His heaven?" The elderly lady replied defiantly, "Yes, because I have been a good person." I slowly informed her that, most certainly, just being a good person would not give her access to heaven but would result in a lost eternity.

Finally, as I realised it might be my last time to ever see this elderly lady, I peered into her eyes and, drawing on a deep compassion, I got down on one knee to plead with her. "I am a young man but even I could die tonight. How much more chance there is of you dying tonight. Mrs Newman, would you please, please give your heart to Jesus?" "Yes, I will," she slowly whispered. My heart welled within me as I led this precious lady to the Lord.

How to lead a person to salvation through Jesus Christ

→ This journey can take five minutes, but also can take a lifetime through building a trusted relationship.

→ Understand you can only lead people where they are willingly to go.

→ Your own life and testimony will be the greatest example you can use.

→ Use eye contact and be sincere with every word.

→ Avoid using biblical terminology which they may not understand.

→ Understand that you are introducing them to a Person, not just a religious faith.

→ Explain what Jesus Christ has saved us from.

→ Explain what Jesus Christ has to offer.

→ Let them ask many questions and never argue.

→ Do not apologise for asking them if they want to accept God's love and thereby enter into a personal relationship with Jesus Christ.

→ If they are willing, pray with them and then encourage them to pray alone.

→ Encourage them to read the Bible, starting at the gospel of John.

→ If possible, recommend a good local church for them and encourage them to get involved.

As our children began to go through their primary school years, I became alarmed at the adverse changes of their attitudes. It seemed like unhealthy attitudes of some school friends were coming into our house and affecting the atmosphere of our home. Drifting off to sleep one night, I was troubled and concerned for my girls and wondered how and when this would stop.

"Don't blame me," that now familiar voice came very sternly. I was shaken and instantly I knew what God meant. I had not been praying over my family as I ought. These principles were deeply impressed on my character. If we know what to do and don't do it, God holds us responsible. He has shown us the way. I always knew that no matter what happens, it is never ever God's fault.

For many nights, after Melonie and Amy were asleep, I would go to their bedrooms and pray over them. Each night I would pray for a heart of worship, a love in them for the Word of God and His presence and that His holy angels would fill the room while the girls slept. Situations were turned around so quickly and in the coming years Melonie and Amy would tell me how they were pretending to sleep but were silently listening each night to my prayers. I learnt to take action when I heard God's voice guiding me as both husband and father.

The voice would come again, "Share your heart with your children." 'But my children know my heart because I preach and tell them a lot of stories,' I thought to myself.

I felt rather insecure as I pondered, 'How do I share my heart with a child? What would I say? How could I start and what would I do?'

"Melonie, tonight we are going to eat out at the best restaurant in town." "Mum coming too?" she asked. "No, just the two of us. Mum and Amy will come another time," I explained. It was fun and a very exciting night with so much to learn on the ways of children. I said she could order whatever she wanted, and Melonie's eyes grew wide. Listening to the Holy Spirit paid off and my children and I became best friends.

"Dad, tell us about the flea that was sitting on the dog's head as he went into Noah's Ark." This was the girls' favourite bedtime story. Another popular tale was the story of

David and Goliath from the perspective of the giant Goliath, as he came to meet David.

They would lay their little hands on my head and pray for blessing as I left on a mission trip. "Dad, I don't want you to go," they sometimes protested. "Okay, I won't go then," I offered. "But Dad, you have to go and tell people about Jesus," they would insist. Coming home from my mission trips abroad, they would jump into my arms until they became too big, and would nearly knock me backwards.

The Holy Spirit is certainly a good teacher, and obeying His guiding voice on being a good father brought enormous dividends in pastoring and a happy family life. The skill of spiritual fatherhood grew in me, alongside that of being a natural father to my children.

13 *Called to a Far Away Land*

||||||||||||||||||||||||||||||||||||||||||||||||||||||||||||||||||||||||||||||||||||||||||||||||||||||||||||||||||||||||||||||||||||||

Beautiful, sandy Mission Beach with views of Dunk Island just across the water is a great place to pray. Summer or winter, the nights are never too cold to stroll along telling Jesus how much you love Him.

Late one night, as I was walking along the beach, a voice spoke to me, "I am going to prune you." "What have I done wrong?" I questioned. The voice came again, "It is not what you have done wrong but what you have done right."

I remembered the scripture about pruning.

"Every branch in Me that does not bear fruit He takes away; and every branch that bears fruit He prunes, that it may bear more fruit."

(John 15:2)

This gave me a nervous assurance that perhaps this 'pruning' might work for the best in the future. Having pruned hundreds of citrus trees in my earlier years, I knew that after the pain of pruning the tree grows bigger and more fruitful.

'Your life is not your own – you were bought with a price' echoed in my heart for many months.

"Do you not know that your body is the temple of the Holy Spirit who is in you, whom you have from God, and you are not your own? For you were bought with a price; therefore glorify God in your body and in your spirit, which are God's."

(1 Corinthians 6:19-20)

These verses were constantly in my thoughts, and I wove them into almost every message I preached in the following six months. However I began to feel as though the Lord had set me up. I felt Him say, "This message is for you."

How to prepare a sermon

→ Choose a subject that you are familiar with and you feel the Holy Spirit wants to convey to the people. Read many scripture passages relating to this subject. Ensure that you have a thorough understanding of sound biblical doctrine on the subject. If in doubt, check your understanding with someone who understands this subject.

→ Use a Bible concordance to do a word search of the key words that portray the content of your sermon.

→ Choose which scriptures you will refer to. They should be the clearest that define what you are saying. List quite a few at first, then narrow them down as you further prepare your sermon.

→ Be careful not to quote scriptures out of context.

→ Ask yourself How, When, Where and Why about the theme of your sermon. This helps you to penetrate the subject. It will also provide relevance of your sermon to listeners and steps to apply in their lives. A good speaker has the ability to make sermons personal to individuals.

→ Write down all thoughts that you have about the subject.

→ *Assemble your written thoughts, eliminating those that don't flow with the main content.*

→ *Depending on how long you have to preach the sermon, have several personal illustrations from your own life that connect with the message. This allows people to relax while you preach and builds a bridge to their hearts.*

→ *Think and pray concerning how you will conclude the sermon, so that the Holy Spirit will continue to move long after you finish speaking.*

→ *Your notes should be abbreviated so that one glance can trigger your thoughts, and you can speak for the next one or two minutes without referring to the notes. This stops your notes from being too wordy and limits the temptation to read your message.*

→ *When the message is prepared, ask yourself, "If I was a person listening to this sermon, what would I receive?" You need to be able to summarize this in one statement.*

→ *Choose a title for your message that is short, catchy and will cause people to be instantly interested when they hear it.*

A week of preaching followed by fishing and scuba diving in the Pacific Islands of Fiji was my preferred time with COC's International President, Pastor Neil Miers. What could be better than enjoying the delicacies of fresh crabs and fish on a Pacific island?

After a week with Neil it felt like a good time to share my heart. Surely he would give guidance if some areas needed pruning. I held back my words, thinking them over carefully before they were ready to come out of my mouth. "Neil, if ever you need to speak into my life about something, I just want you to know that I give you that right." I spoke seriously, and there was an awkward silence before Neil responded slowly, "I have been waiting a long time for this day." My heart sank as my mind raced with many thoughts, 'Why did I say it, and what have I done wrong? What has Neil been waiting to correct?' "When the crabs come on the table, you eat far too many," Neil chuckled. "Don't worry, I'll let you know."

Wanting to move the conversation along, I asked how the work was going in England. A few years before, several couples had left Australia to found churches in England and Europe, and I had not heard much about their progress. "We need a father from Australia to go and oversee the work," Neil said thoughtfully. We discussed a few other countries and then conversation shifted to the passing scenery.

That night in a Fijian hotel room in Nadi (pronounced 'Nandi'), I felt a spiritual restlessness, troubled by Neil's words earlier in the day. Is the work in England being held up because there are not enough fathers? I was gripped by this thought. The more I dwelt on this I became excited, challenged and somewhat insecure that maybe God was calling me. 'But surely not,' I reasoned, 'Ruth and I are very busy where we are.'

Arriving back in Innisfail, I was deep in thought. Could God be moving us on? Could it be England? Stopping at a traffic light, I suddenly felt I had to get it off my chest. "I think God might be moving us to the other side of the world," I muttered quickly. Briefly I looked over to see Ruth's response. She sat quietly with her head bowed. I had been through China that year and Ruth later told me that she first thought I was going to say that God was calling us to China. "Where?" Ruth asked in surprise. "To England," I said hesitantly. The rest of the car journey was fairly subdued. Ruth told me later that when I said 'England,' she knew in her heart that it must be God calling us.

How to preach a sermon

→ Pray and yield your whole body to the Holy Spirit for Him to use the words you speak. *Always remember that preaching the sermon is not about you but rather about other people and their walk with God.*

→ Be aware of the time that you are given and approximate how far you should be through your message at regular intervals, i.e., one third, two thirds.

→ Relax and walk confidently to the pulpit.

→ Do not apologise for lack of time to prepare or what you have to say.

→ Publicly honour and appreciate the person who is the leader of that particular group or church.

→ Smile and look across the people as you slowly and enthusiastically speak from your heart, introducing your sermon topic.

→ When you read the scriptures, do so with clarity and expression.

→ During the course of the sermon use eye contact and slowly move naturally and relaxed, connecting with everyone.

→ Remember that you are not just preaching to a crowd, but many individuals. Everyone is important and wants to see your eyes towards them at some point.

→ Use voice modulation and expression to engage with people.

→ Remember that people live by seeing pictures. In your personal illustrations or Bible stories endeavour to paint a picture in people's minds.

→ Avoid looking at an individual when making a statement that could be viewed as negative to that person.

→ Never preach a message to correct a certain person in the group or church. If your eyes cross a person who you know has a certain problem that you have just mentioned, do not linger on that thought or person.

→ Stick to your plan of preaching the sermon in the allocated time. If you are running behind at your predetermined point of one third and two thirds, you will need to shorten the remaining points and illustrations so as to stay within your time.

→ As you near the end, don't wind down in your passion for the message but rather bring it to a decision-making climax in the closing minutes.

→ At the close of your sermon, if at all possible, give the opportunity for people to accept Christ as their Saviour.

The following week I asked Neil, "Do you think God is calling us to England?" He raised his eyebrows and announced, "God hasn't said anything to me." 'What a relief,' I thought, 'it was all in my mind!' Then Neil suggested, "Go on a mission trip to England and see what you feel."

Over the following weeks Ruth became increasingly convinced that God was calling us. It was quite difficult keeping this as a secret from Melonie and Amy. We were responsible for their wellbeing and security, so wanted to be totally sure of our decision before breaking the news to our girls. We wanted them to visit the UK first, so that they would have some familiarity with the land where we might one day live.

In September 1992 our family spent two weeks travelling through the few churches in the UK. I saw people in London. They looked grey, miserable and so lacking in life that I prayed, "Lord, I want to put a smile on their faces and some colour back into those English people." It was fairly cloudy, so maybe these people had not seen sun for some time.

Arriving back in Australia, I felt obsessed with England and kept praying for those people and their nation.

In January 1993 Neil Miers telephoned me. "Do you still feel like going to England?" "Yes, I think about the place every day," I admitted. It had been many months since we discussed England. "Well, pack your bags and go," Neil said. I took the phone from my ear and stared at the receiver. "What did you say? Did God or you change your mind?" I asked. "I knew it was God all the time but wanted you to know for sure," he said. Then Neil went on, "You will find some demons in England and then you will really need to know that God has sent you. It will be no good saying to the demons that Neil sent you – you have got to know that God sent you!" I put the phone down and my mind started to race. Our new house had to be sold. 'Where will we live, and who do we tell?' Each answer was followed by hundreds more questions. 'Where do we begin?' I wondered. We had to tell our girls first.

My daughters, Melonie and Amy, have two very different personalities and the news of our moving brought two very different responses. Melonie jumped up with a shout and gasp and barricaded herself in the bathroom, while Amy sat still with a sad look on her face, asking about her cat.

"When Mum and I left the farm you were small and didn't have to use your faith because you were covered by ours," I explained to the girls. "Now it is very different and you can exercise your faith that God will bless you as you put your trust in Him."

I travelled through Vanuatu and the Solomon Islands, saying goodbye to all my wonderful South Pacific Island friends, and everywhere I went I wondered if we would ever meet again. There were no tears when our house was sold, but there were many as I waved goodbye to these people who had become a part of my life.

In May 1993, one month before the Schmierer family were due to board flights to London, something happened that people would talk of for years to come.

About thirty leaders of the Australian Christian Outreach Centre churches had gathered together at a camp site on the outskirts of Brisbane. It was Monday, and the day before some extraordinary things had happened in the Sunday meetings. There was talk that people had been stuck on the floor – some had seen visions and some had laughed for hours. It all sounded rather strange for those, like me, who had not been present at the Brisbane Sunday meetings. "Yes. Well, we had a good Sunday in our church too," I assured them, feeling slightly disconnected.

A Rugby League game was watched before the meeting. A few men complained that this was not very spiritual, especially in light of the Holy Spirit moving so mightily the day before. Most of the men opted to watch this State of Origin game. For this match, each player returns to play for the Australian State in which he was born. Every Aussie is familiar with this annual match and New South Wales won it that night. Being mainly Queenslanders, we jumped on the only New South Welshman present.

At ten o'clock in the evening, games aside, it was time to worship God. Pastor Neil Miers spoke for a few minutes on how he had recently seen God do amazing, supernatural things. Then he said, "Who knows? Maybe God might do something tonight."

We began to sing a song, "Holy Ghost, You're wonderful," and a beautiful, tangible presence of God filled the room. Three hours later, most men were on the floor, some laughing and others were seeing visions. A few were spectators, but all were amazed at what was happening. None doubted that this was a fresh outpouring of the Holy Spirit, just like the first outpouring on the day of Pentecost, recorded in the book of Acts.

*All were amazed and perplexed, saying to one another,
"Whatever could this mean?" Others, mocking, said,
"They are full of new wine." But Peter, standing up with
the eleven, raised his voice and said to them, "Men of
Judea and all who dwell in Jerusalem, let this be known to
you, and heed my words. For these are not drunk as you
suppose, since it is only the third hour of the day. But this
is what was spoken by the prophet Joel: 'And it shall come
to pass in the last days, says God, that I will pour out of
My Spirit on all flesh. Your sons and your daughters shall
prophesy. Your young men shall see visions, your old men
shall dream dreams.'"*

(Acts 2:12-17)

That night, crawling down the path that led to the
dormitories, I passed various men who felt too intoxicated
by the Holy Spirit to walk. These men, like me, were totally
overwhelmed by the Spirit of God. Some of those more
intoxicated by the Holy Spirit lay in the grass and others
on bench seats outside the dormitories. It was indeed a
night to remember. People were laughing even as they went
to sleep.

For three days we met together and, occasionally, I was
carried off and put to bed. Drunk with the presence of God,
I had difficulty walking for those three days. I had never in
my life been drunk with alcohol, and had certainly never
before experienced this with the Holy Spirit. This event was
unique and changed my life forever.

Each day I saw visions of what God was doing and what He
wanted to do. He showed me visions of Europe – of people and
nations I had never seen before. Two significant visions became
so embedded in me that they profoundly affected my life.

In one such vision I saw a map of Europe before my eyes.
I felt the Lord say, "Take your fist and hit the map." I did,

and there before me appeared a red dot on Britain. He said, "Hit the map again." Another red dot appeared. I realised that these dots represented cities where churches would be established. He said, "Take your other fist and hit the map." A red dot appeared on the continent of Europe. "Hit the map again," the Lord continued. Again I hit the map. "More and faster," the word came. Both my fists began to move as fast as they could, hitting the map at random all over continental Europe and Britain. Red dots appeared everywhere and I heard once more, "Faster, for the time is short!" These were cities opening up to revival! The map became red with dots before me. Europe would be touched and changed as cities became affected by this amazing move of God's Spirit.

I said, "Lord, show me some of these people of Britain who You will give me." Before my eyes I saw a group of scraggly, sickly, grey people. Their arms hung down as though depressed. Their faces were sad and lonely. I was shocked and questioned, "Lord, is this all that You are going to give me when I go to Europe?" He replied, "Watch and see." I then saw the wind of God's Spirit blow across those miserable people and they were transformed before me. Their arms and heads were lifted up. Their faces began to smile. Their chests came out and their chins were held high. I said eagerly, "Lord, give me those scraggly people."

Over the years these visions became reality, as Ruth and I moved to the United Kingdom and established churches across Europe. We have seen God transform thousands of people's lives across Europe and beyond.

In the following weeks, churches across Australia were touched by this fresh move of God. Many miracles occurred, as lives were changed and empowered by this fresh outpouring.

What do you preach on the first Sunday after such an encounter with the Holy Spirit?

That Sunday in May, the morning church service went on for six hours, as people felt stuck to the floor and could not move. It was an outpouring of God's Spirit, the like of which most had never seen before. At each meeting over the next month, unusual things happened, and even after we left for Britain it continued for most of the next year. God had come with supernatural joy and power to refresh His Church.

House sold, we needed our car right up until the last days before leaving Australia, but now we had to sell it quickly. I left our room in the hotel with a sheet of white cardboard, a marker pen, scissors and tape to put a sign on the windscreen.

Absorbed in making my sign, I started to affix the card to the window. I did not notice a man walking up to the car. "You won't need that sign." Raising my head, I asked, "What do you mean?" "I'm buying it!" "Don't you need to test drive it?" I quizzed this mystery man. "No, I don't need to." With that, he wrote out a cheque and drove the car away. A few minutes after I had left the hotel with my cardboard, pen, scissors and tape, I walked back inside, holding a cheque. Ruth asked, "Did you forget something?" "It's sold! The car is gone." It had all happened so quickly!

In Cairns airport, Ruth, our girls and I filled out the emigration departure form to leave Australia. "Will we depart temporarily or permanently? Which should we tick?" "Let's depart permanently." We laughed and boarded our flight, bound for the United Kingdom.

14 *A Place South of London*

Arriving at London Heathrow on the 8th of June 1993, the Schmierer family were prepared for the adventure of a lifetime.

The United Kingdom, a distinctive island nation in Western Europe, is a conglomerate of States. England, Scotland and Wales are known together as Great Britain. Add Northern Ireland and there you have it – the United Kingdom of Great Britain and Northern Ireland – boasting a population of more than sixty million. All of these people fit into a land mass slightly smaller than the US state of Oregon, just under half the size of France and thirty times smaller than Australia.

Britain's legislators work hard to protect the countryside. Densely populated cities merge in a blink of an eye into rolling green fields neatly hemmed by manicured hedges. They stand in stark contrast to Australia's vast, sunburnt, rough and ragged landscape.

As I wandered up to the supermarket's delicatessen counter, waiting to be served, an orchestra of throat-clearing and foot shuffling erupted somewhere behind my right shoulder. "Excuse me, Sir. There is a queue." Was someone talking to me? "A what?" I turned and looked back to see a long line of people, many of whom seemed rather displeased. I tried to explain that I didn't have time to wait, but this was not well received. I had rarely seen queues in Australia, and decided that the English were the most patient people on earth.

Soon after arriving in Britain, we took a ferry to Europe to visit some of the churches there. As the ferry pulled away from the port of Dover, we watched the famous white cliffs growing smaller on the horizon.

On the ferry we struck up a conversation with a British woman who asked why we had come to Britain. I answered, "To start new churches." She looked bewildered. "Don't you think there are enough churches here already?" She explained, "They're on most street corners." 'Not enough,' I thought. 'Britain needs more churches with a vision to raise up Christian leaders and where the Holy Spirit is passionately sought after.'

In one day we could drive through France, Belgium, Holland and Germany, crossing a national border every few hours. People of so many nations and cultures lived so close together with barely distinguishable borders between them. I collected stamps as a child and treasured those from these distant countries of Old Europe. Foreign cities and landmarks felt curiously familiar to this rural Australian.

The world seemed so close and my Australian farmer's life so far away. I travelled through various cities of Britain and experienced the variety of its ethnic diversity. In one street I could be in India, yet in another street in the Middle East. So many cultures so intrinsically different, all living together. Like us, so many people had immigrated and now called Great Britain their home, each with a story to tell.

Where would we go and which city would be our home? We had many questions and few answers. Ruth and I knew that God had called us to this old land for a new move of God's Spirit. However, the rest of the details were far less clear.

The Lord had spoken before leaving Australia, "Some place south of London and in the first two months I will show you where." When I received this word, it sounded quite specific. There couldn't be that many places south of London, after all. On our arrival in Britain we bought a car and a musical keyboard and drove to any town in which God opened a door. At times I felt like Abraham who had left his land, wandering around looking for a new home, while at other times I felt like Peter walking on the water and trusting Jesus. We found that there were so many places south of London.

Adjusting to life in a new country

→ *If the weather can be harsh, it is best to arrive when it is a mild time of year, so as to give time to adjust.*

→ *It is best to rent a house rather than buy, so as to get your bearings concerning the best area in which to live.*

→ *Get your family registered with a medical doctor and understand what is covered by your insurance.*

→ *Ensure that your driver's licence is converted to a licence for that country. Usually you will have only a certain length of time to do this.*

→ *Pay attention to the different driving and car parking rules.*

→ *Get an accountant's advice on personal taxation laws that will be applicable to you.*

→ *Give special attention to each of your family members who individually will need to adjust in their own time. Build an atmosphere of joy in your home.*

→ *Build relationships. People may be able to connect you with their friends, relatives or acquaintances in your new country.*

→ Don't always compare your homeland with your new country. It will irritate your new friends.

→ Stay focused on your purpose. If you dwell on romantic feelings towards your old country, you will never become settled in your new country. Your thoughts will affect the way you feel.

→ Choose to call your new country 'home'!

Driving around London's M25 ring road, I requested of God that there be a group of people waiting for us, and ideally a building near a railway station. By now we were weary of traffic jams and thought perhaps people could come to church meetings by train. Six weeks after arriving in Britain we were given a phone number of some people near Brighton who had been meeting together to pray. We looked at the map and found that Brighton was directly south of London, although perhaps too far south.

We discovered that the Holy Spirit moved on polite British people in the same way as Australians, and people laughed on the floor as the Holy Spirit moved. The next morning Ruth and I returned to Swindon, a city west of London where we had temporarily based ourselves. That night the Lord spoke to us about Brighton. "In that city I have many bruised, hurt, misunderstood, and scattered people who I want you to gather and train." This was the direction from God that I had sought.

The first Sunday was a relaxed meeting in a house and the Holy Spirit fell again. Praying for one woman, I felt that her spiritual pulse had almost stopped. "God is quickening your pulse and you will not die, but you will be young again," I prophesied. The following week this woman's daughter would tell me that living in her parents' house felt like living in a morgue. God transformed this woman so much that sixteen years later she seemed younger and more vibrant than ever, leading the children's ministry across the city of Brighton. There was an innocence and excitement that God was surely on the move. We discovered that this group of people in Brighton had started meeting together to pray in the very month that God had spoken to me in Australia to come to Britain. God had directed us and we had found each other from the opposite sides of the planet!

During the following week the momentum grew and those present at the house meeting invited friends who were thirsty for God. On the second Sunday we rented a small hotel room that seated sixty people.

"How many communion glasses will we need? Let's ask God for a word of knowledge." I said thoughtfully, "Perhaps fifteen or twenty?" Ruth confidently announced, "Your faith is too small." Ruth was correct. By now, the 15th of August 1993, in the middle of English summer holidays, forty people came in the morning and sixty in the evening without any advertising. God was moving mightily and many thirsty British people flocked to be touched by God.

On the third Sunday sixty people would attend in the morning and 120 in the evening and this was still a sixty-seat room. These were the hungriest people we had ever seen and God was meeting them in their area of need. People crammed into the room, while others peered over their heads from the steps and out into the corridors. Many people appeared drunk, just as in Acts chapter two when the Holy Spirit moved on the day of Pentecost. Consequently, some people were carried from the hotel and put in cars to be driven home.

How to have a move of God's Spirit – bring these two principles together:

Learn and work with the ways of God

→ Someone must pay the price to know God, walk closely with Him and be confident in His presence. There is always a 'somebody' God uses to initiate moves of His Spirit.

He made known His ways unto Moses, His acts to the children of Israel. (Psalm 103:7)

→ Earnestly and consistently pray for God to come and move upon your life, church and city. This may take months or even years, but always expect Him to come in His power.

→ Find others with this same passion, praying with them and hopefully some church leaders will join you. It is always easier when church leaders are involved.

→ The local church leadership should not grieve the Holy Spirit.

→ Honour His presence by giving the Holy Spirit time and room to move.

→ Obey what the Holy Spirit says through His humble, experienced and anointed servants.

Learn and work with the ways of people

→ Understand the culture of the people you are trying to reach.

→ Love these people and genuinely care for them. If they become offended, their hearts will be closed to you, making it more difficult for God to touch them.

→ Arouse the spiritual hunger of people by gently bringing them to a place where they can see their need for more of God in their lives.

One day an Englishman came to our house for encouragement. We spoke together about the things of God and I asked if he wanted me to pray for him before he left. He had heard that the Holy Spirit could move so powerfully that often people were left unable to drive, and so declined my invitation. He excused himself and explained. "No, I have to drive home, but could I use your restroom before I go?" I pointed the direction to the bathroom, and a few minutes later heard a crashing noise coming from that direction. Ruth and I looked at each other, wondering what was happening in there. The bathroom door opened slowly and the man crawled out on his knees. Staring up at us, the Englishman said, "He is in there, the Holy Ghost is in there." He struggled to stand up and made his way to the door. Without looking back he reached his car, unlocked it, and sat for some time in the driver's seat. This was indeed a mighty outpouring of the Holy Spirit as God baptised people afresh in His glory.

In the following weeks the hotel rooms became too small, as God drew people from all over the South East of England. These included many outstanding leaders who felt in transition and were looking for a new church home. We invited a few of these potential leaders to our home each Wednesday evening to be trained.

One night a well spoken couple, David and Jackie Harland, were amongst them. As Ruth led worship from the keyboard, the Holy Spirit came amongst the people and they began to fall to the floor under the power of God. David and Jackie were left standing as Ruth also slid to the floor behind the keyboard. David whispered to his wife, Jackie, "I think it is time for us to leave." I noticed them stepping over people, heading for the door and said, "Excuse me, sir, could I pray for you before you go?" David braced himself but he quickly fell under God's power. This nice Englishman was conquered by the Holy Spirit and several years later became

*Ashley and Ruth with their training pastors, Kevin and Bev Dales,
Innisfail, Australia*

*Youth leaders, Ashley and Ruth, with Innisfail Youth
at the summit of Mt. Tyson, Tully*

Ashley with Levi and Melody Lauasi and the church people at Mt. Zion, Malaita, Solomon Islands

Ashley with Neil Miers (right) and student, Solomon Islands

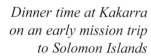

Dinner time at Kakarra on an early mission trip to Solomon Islands

Ashley dedicates babies, Solomon Islands

Ministry Training School Principal for eight years – Murray Townsend with Ashley, Solomon Islands

Ashley with people of the Western Province, Solomon Islands

Ministry Training School graduation, Solomon Islands

Ashley with Timon Gao (centre back) and other pastors, Vanuatu

Ashley preaches at open-air conference, Solomon Islands

Called by God to the United Kingdom – Ashley at Westminster, London

Ashley visits the grave of reformer John Wesley, London

London Marathon 2005 – Ashley in crowd of runners, and crossing the finish line

The building at Brighton, owned by CityCoast Church, Christian Outreach Centre's UK base

One of many regional training schools, Ukraine

Ashley with people testifying to outstanding healings, Ukraine: Gregory, given only days to live and healed from cancer; Rutislav healed from paralysis and numerous other diseases

Ashley, camel rider, Egypt

Ashley and Randeep Mathews (on right) at a Sikh village after an outdoor meeting where many miracles occurred, India

Fakhry Hanna with Ashley, Egypt

Ashley and David Harland, minister to many, India

*Pastors and leaders at Himalayan
conference, Nepal*

*Ashley with Nepal's
Prime Minister, Mr Koirala*

*Ashley and Ruth with
David Harland (left)
and Raju Sundas (right)
(Himalaya mountains
behind), Nepal*

*Ashley at Balkans conference
in Plovdiv, Bulgaria, with
Bojidar and Toni Simeonov,
Rodja Orescanin of Serbia
and Julian Melfi of London*

the senior pastor of this new dynamic church that God had created in Brighton.

Brighton is famous for several things. It has an Indian-style palace built by the Prince Regent in the 1800's, a monument to the variety and opulence of the 19th century British Empire. Brighton's beach does not have sand but is famous for its pebbles. History records that in June 1865 Britain's well known missionary, Hudson Taylor, was walking along this pebbled beach when God called him to the people of China.

In more recent times, at 2:54am on the 12th of October 1984, the Irish Republican Army (IRA) attempted to assassinate the British Prime Minister, Margaret Thatcher, at the Grand Hotel in Brighton. The bomb caused huge destruction to the hotel with several fatalities and injuries but Margaret Thatcher, or as some called her 'The Iron Lady', survived.

It was so exciting to have found the place where God had called us to establish a new church and to begin the work of training church leaders for Britain. Only an hour away was London Heathrow, the busiest international airport in the world. Within two hours' drive from Brighton over twenty million people lived – the population of the whole of Australia! Everything was so close and I decided there would be no shortage of people to welcome into our church.

Now we had to get down to day to day living in a foreign land. Where would we live and where would the children go to school? The church was already gathering people through the hotel meetings. But we were still grappling with the challenges of living in a different culture. In the country towns of Australia, people usually acknowledged one another as they passed in the street. Going for a walk down the streets of Brighton, I tried to be friendly. "Good day! How are you? Hello!" I greeted various passersby. Most people lowered their heads as though to make themselves anonymous and invisible. Years later, watching a film in which Crocodile Dundee visited New York, I knew exactly how he felt.

Founding a new church

→ *Pray and seek God for His plan for this new church.*

→ *Try to find those people who are praying for something new in the city. Usually, God has prepared some people to join a new church.*

→ *Don't ask people to join your new church but leave it to God to speak to them.*

→ *Form a functional team with the people you have.*

→ *Identify what you have to offer people – what are your and your team's strengths? Thereby, decide the emphasis of your new church.*

→ *Regularly speak about who is your spiritual oversight. It gives people security to know that you are under another church leader's authority. It is good if that leader can come and speak in your church, regardless of congregation numbers.*

→ *People are attracted to vision. So at every meeting speak about your vision, of which an important part must be to reach those who don't yet know Christ.*

→ *Spend a lot of time building relationships with as many local people as possible.*

→ *Every pastor will have his/her own ways of doing things, but be yourself. Don't behave in a certain way just to try to get people to join your church.*

→ *Honour other pastors who have led or are presently leading churches in your local area.*

→ *Ensure the building and your meetings are covered by public liability insurance.*

Through wisdom a house is built, and by understanding it is established.

(Proverbs 24:3)

"Is your church going to be a middle class or working class church?" someone asked. I was startled, as I hadn't heard of such a thing before. Over the coming week I was asked the same question twice more, one middle class woman informing me, "There are five of us in your church." I thought, 'What an odd distinction to make.' Because we had come from outside the British class system, people were not sure how to categorise us.

One popular song that we sang at most meetings was 'We're gonna take this land in the name of the Lord.' I was enjoying the prophetic flavour of the song when a nice woman spoke up, "Excuse me. In England we say that we are going to take this land!" I chuckled, "Sorry lady, we haven't got that much time."

In a city that attracts many conferences, it was difficult to keep a constant booking in a hotel ballroom. Finally we found an accommodating hotel as the church began to explode in growth. The Holy Spirit fell in each meeting with various manifestations. One evening several elderly guests sat sipping tea in the hotel foyer, as our new church members were carried past, merrily under the influence of the Holy Spirit, arms and legs akimbo. The next morning the hotel manager asked to meet me for a little chat. This gentleman gestured to me to sit in the foyer and muttered, "I am very pleased you are meeting with a lot of success but you are changing the atmosphere of my hotel. I am sorry but you will have to find another venue." I begged for a few weeks' grace but none were forthcoming.

Our next door neighbour was quite an intelligent man, and a director of a large international company. One day he asked me something which had clearly been bothering him. "Ashley, you say that you started your church in a hotel? How did you get the bricks and stones in every Sunday to have your meetings?" He thought that each Sunday we constructed a stone church building in the hotel and there we had our meeting. We had many committed workers but not quite enough to construct an entire building each week! My neighbour did not understand that a church could be anything different than a few people inside an old, stone building with a steeple.

God had come with His amazing grace and brought a fresh breath of His presence to many lives. His words to me – 'In that city I have many, bruised, hurt, misunderstood, and scattered people who I want you to gather and train' – were coming true. We moved each week from hotel to hotel, but now our focus was to find a building to lease so that the next stage of God's amazing plan could be fulfilled.

15 *Believe Me or Pack Your Bags*

Before we came to Brighton I had asked God for 'a group of people waiting for us and a building next to a railway station.' We had found the people waiting for us and maybe now the building was also in sight. A large warehouse only one hundred metres from the Hove railway station would be our leased venue. We applied to the council for planning permission to use it for our church worship, offices and training centre.

I was surprised to receive a phone call from the Mayor of the city. It was the afternoon before the councillors were due to debate our application to use the warehouse as a place of worship. "Are you Pastor Schmierer?" "Yes sir, I am," I responded, as my mind raced. "I am ringing to say that I won't vote for you tomorrow," he informed me, trying to sound sincere. Absolutely devastated, I called two friends and asked them to pray. Despondently I paced the house and complained to God, "Why? This is not fair. They didn't do this to me in Australia. I have given up so much to be here. Why?"

Our growing church had put all their hopes towards getting this building and now it looked like we had been beaten. Closing the door, I walked slowly back and forth in the room. "If you are not going to believe Me, then pack your bags and go back to Australia," I felt God speak to my heart. "Oh God, I can't go back to Australia! We have just arrived." "Believe me!" He insisted.

The next morning I woke up early to pray and believe God for His favour at the council meeting.

The Lord brought Mark 11:22-23 to my mind: *"Have faith in God. For assuredly, I say to you, whoever says to this mountain, 'Be removed and cast into the sea,' and does not doubt in his heart, but believes that those things he says will be done, he will have whatever he says."*

I began praying fervently for this problem (or mountain) to be cast into the sea. In our home I prayed loudly and passionately and saw the obstacle sinking deeper into the depths of the sea. Later as I came to breakfast, Ruth said, "I listened to the news this morning and the oceans are rising!" "Wow! Is this global warming?" I asked. "No." Ruth said with a smile, "A mountain has been cast into the sea this morning!"

Later in the day we took our positions in the visitors' gallery of the council chambers where we could view and listen to every word of the deliberations. The council meeting was very formal and with each and every application the councillors deliberated and scrutinised every little detail. My heart was nervous but remained steadfast with the word God had spoken, "If you are not going to believe Me, then pack your bags and go back to Australia. Believe Me!"

As our application was opened before the councillors, we watched carefully the expressions on their faces and particularly that of the Mayor. One councillor volunteered, "I have a little church next to me and they are wonderful people." Then another added, "I have heard these people are noisy. My question is, how noisy can they be when we have a football stadium in the middle of this city?" Another opined, "I think these people should be able to go to church in the middle of town." Suddenly the whole atmosphere had changed. The clerk said, "All those in favour raise your hand." Everyone raised hands except for the Mayor. Then, as he glanced around, he sheepishly raised his hand and made the vote unanimous. God had indeed cast the mountain into the sea and had once again been faithful to His word. A team of willing workers quickly renovated this unused warehouse into a meeting place for worshippers. We knew this was only a temporary building, but were so happy to have a home base for our many operations.

Over the next few months many men asked me, "Will you be my father?" This echoed in my heart. Many years before, it was prophesied about me, "You will be a father to the fatherless and indeed a father in the gospel." The Lord had also been faithful and clear in His words, "In that city I have many, bruised, hurt, misunderstood, and scattered people who I want you to gather and train."

One morning I came down to our church warehouse to find the outside door unlocked. Entering the building, I could hear someone inside. To get a better view of whoever had broken into our building, I cautiously moved to get a view. In the auditorium I found Lee, our caretaker, praying fervently as he walked along the platform. Lee could not see me but I could hear every word. I stood there and listened with shock and amazement to the prayers he was praying. This man spoke the exact words that I had prayed many years before while walking on a beach in Australia. This young man was one of those God had shown me before coming to Britain – a group of scraggly, sickly, people with their arms hanging down as though depressed, with faces grey, sad and lonely. In my vision I had seen the wind of God's Spirit blow across these miserable people until they were transformed before me. Their arms and heads were lifted up, and their faces began to smile. Lee became one of those who would be trained and many years later his father encouraged me, "Ashley, you have done for my son what I could not do myself."

An hour's drive west of Brighton is the city of Portsmouth. I have stood on Portsmouth's beach from which, over two hundred years before, convicts were sent to 'New South Wales', or 'Australia' as this land would later be named. This happened in the latter part of the 18th century and some convicts were only children, sent to a distant, harsh land, never to return to their homeland. I have also seen the Port Arthur convict settlement in Tasmania where convicts were incarcerated and often died. They, like the native Aborigines who had inhabited Australia for millennia, endured enormous grief and pain. This pain, particularly in the case of the Aborigines, has taken many generations to heal.

Despite these painful origins, the bond between Australia and Britain is very deep, and kindred spirits coupled with a fierce rivalry in sport has wrought an unusual relationship.

As a boy, the stories of the British pioneers who had left their homeland two centuries ago had captivated my heart. Every school child in Australia studies in detail the progress of various early explorers who led expeditions into its uncharted regions.

These explorers such Leichardt, Burke and Wills courageously opened up the land for others to come and settle. Blaxland, Lawson and Wentworth were the first Europeans to cross the rough terrain of the Blue Mountains, west of Sydney. As a boy growing up in rural Australia, in my mind these men were more famous than any pop idol or sporting hero. I loved adventure and sometimes wondered if there were any new lands left to explore.

Since coming to Brighton, United Kingdom, I have thought many times of what the early British pioneers in Australia possessed and endured, and of the life they left behind. They had a dream to conquer the horizon and they forged the way for others – the settlers who came when life was more comfortable. Maybe some of their wives cried, "Take me home. You didn't tell me it was going to be like this. There is not even a kitchen here, let alone an oven!"

Ruth and I came with our dream to Britain. We were pioneers together and never once did Ruth ever complain about what she had given up, even though she could not be in Australia for the death of her father. In Britain God gave us a team who began dreaming of towns and cities, places where we were to explore and establish new churches.

The attitude of a pioneer

→ Keep continual passion for your cause.

→ Maintain a consistent and disciplined prayer life.

→ Build resilience and determination that will carry you past the point where others stop.

→ Long-term vision – always keep the end picture in sight.

→ Clarify your current position.

→ Strategic planning will take you from where you are to where you dream to be.

The Brighton church quickly became established as a strong local church in the community. However, this was only the first of many newly established churches in God's plan.

In 1994 we established a Ministry Training School for those who felt the call of God towards full time ministry. The focus on training and outreach saw churches founded in Brighton and three other towns within the first year. The British pioneering spirit was waiting to be roused again. We met many who wanted to preach the gospel, but were just waiting for someone to train and help them fulfil their ministry calling.

God spoke to me about the city of Aberdeen, Scotland, "I have resources in this city for all of Scotland." However, at that stage I was not even sure precisely where Aberdeen was on the map. Also known as the Granite City, Aberdeen is the heart of North Sea oil production. It is a Scottish city, but oil workers come from all over the world, making it a very multicultural city. Towards the end of one of our training schools, a young English couple, Kevin and Cheryl, told us that although they had never been there, they felt called to Aberdeen.

With their young children they moved north to Scotland. As they approached Aberdeen, Cheryl began to weep with a love and compassion for the city that they had never seen before. As real pioneers, this was a great adventure for them. They soon gathered many people to that vision. In only a few years their new church owned a building and they, too, trained and sent out pioneering pastors into other cities of Scotland.

To me, these will forever be modern heroes of the faith who pioneered and made a way for others to follow. They, like the first disciples of Christ, went out to bring life and hope to individuals, towns and cities.

Once as I was on the phone to the Australian airline, Qantas, while on hold I found myself listening to the programmed music. As I waited, the song was being played, 'I still call Australia home.' The words were so romantic and soothing, and my mind drifted with the spirit of the song. Abruptly I realised where those words were leading me, and that Australia was no longer my home. I pulled the receiver from my ear and spoke into it, "Get behind me, Satan," and hung up with a flourish. Ruth and I had fallen in love with Britain and this land was now our home.

16 *Feed the Bear*

I glanced over the letter, sighed, and threw it on the 'read' pile of mail. 'Ashley,' it began, 'a good time for you to visit the Ukraine would be March 1996.' It was already early March and I didn't like feeling pushed. As I turned to give attention to other papers, I heard God say, "Pick it back up. I will give you the resources to affect this nation." Startled, I grabbed the letter and read it thoroughly several times, wondering at its request and the word that God had just spoken.

Within two weeks I found myself in the Ukraine with one of our UK pastors, meeting our recommended contacts. I shared that God had spoken to me about affecting their nation. This was greeted with a mixture of interest and cynicism. "We have heard the same from many western pastors when they arrive in the Ukraine," came the sceptical response from one senior Ukrainian leader. "Many come, take their photos and then leave. Show us by your actions." As we travelled to the airport and then returned to London, my thoughts lingered on the pastor's words, and I wondered how I could keep my word to these Ukrainian pastors.

The Ukraine's story is that of a people toughened by hardship and wars. The former Soviet Union's impact on this nation is seen everywhere. The hammer and sickle emblem still remains above many public venues and offices.

These proud, hard working people, savagely oppressed by many conquering armies, made a stand for independence on the 24th of August 1991 and were officially recognised by the international community as a sovereign nation the same year on the 25th of December.

The Ukraine had been called the 'Bread Basket of the Soviet Union' and was renowned for the rich variety of agricultural crops it produced. However, millions of its people died in the forced famines initiated by the Soviet regime in order to teach this strong-willed nation to submit to its authority. Countless numbers also died in the Siberian labour camps under this same cruel regime.

During the years of communism many Ukrainians were convinced that the Western governments led by America might attack their nation at any moment. The Soviet Union also had their plans to retaliate. Gennadiy, one of my Ukrainian friends who I came to work with, had been a colonel in the Russian Army and once found himself in a planning meeting for a Soviet invasion of Australia. When I was a teenager, while our Australian soldiers were fighting in Vietnam, I had nightmares and woke up fearful that communists had surrounded our farmhouse. Decades later, it felt strange indeed to be preaching alongside formerly devout communists who were now passionate to know the true and living God.

The Chernobyl power station accident of 1986 and subsequent radiation contamination caused many in the vicinity to live with lingering health problems. On my second visit in 1996 I preached in the nearby city and afterwards was treated to the usual Ukrainian hospitality of a tasty bowl of hot borsch soup. I gave thanks to God for the food with a bit more faith and fervour than usual, especially when I was told that watermelons from the region had set off metal detectors due to radiation absorbed by the fruit ten years after the original accident.

It was a bleak night and the blizzard drove the snow horizontally across our path. The trip from Chernobyl to Kiev was going to be dangerous. Occasionally the car skidded and I quietly prayed, "Lord, my life is in your hands, not the driver's tonight." God had spoken to my heart about the Ukraine but where and how could this happen? I spoke no Russian.

"Feed the bear!" Later I heard that God had already spoken these words into Rob Smillie's heart in the early 1990's. He could have looked in the nearest zoo for an undernourished bear, but fortunately Rob recognised this as a direction to learn to speak Russian so he could one day give 'the bear' (the former Soviet Union) the food that would eternally satisfy.

How to stir leadership gifts in others

→ *People with a strong anointing upon their own life will impact the hearts and callings of others.*

→ *Encourage people to aspire to leadership, and show them it is worth the effort.*

→ *People desire to lead when they see a role in which they are needed, and where they can persevere and thereby make a difference.*

→ *Encourage people to study and be good at what they do in society (i.e., family, government, education, arts & entertainment, media, religion, business).*

→ *There are many different leadership styles. Honour other leaders who have a different style to your own. This encourages people to be themselves.*

→ *Consistently promote teamwork in projects. Leadership is about engaging with a group of people to get a job done.*

→ *Share the victories that you have experienced personally. More importantly, celebrate the successes of others.*

In the coming years, Rob and I with many of our United Kingdom pastors would make many trips, investing much in resources to host regional pastors' and leaders' training schools across the Ukraine. In a few years more than thirty regional training schools had gathered over 5,000 pastors and leaders from across many denominations and every region of the Ukraine.

Our Ukraine accommodation was usually a communist-era apartment flat. All of these apartment blocks are served by the same rattling, dark elevators in which every shudder and clunk feels as though it will be the last. This gives a recurring and curious feeling that they are never serviced.

The Pavlograd meetings were in a theatre with the seating gradually rising towards the back and there was a large stage from which we spoke. Every seat was occupied, as pastors and leaders from many denominations were present. Just after 9am there was some praise and worship followed by prayer before the first session of teaching.

I glanced across to acknowledge some of my Ukrainian friends. As usual, broad smiles decorated with gold teeth smiled back in return. Older Ukrainians invested their wealth in the form of gold teeth during the communist era because it would be safe from being stolen.

I took the microphone and began to pray for a short time in tongues as recorded in Acts 2:4. *And they were all filled with the Holy Spirit and began to speak with other tongues, as the Spirit gave them utterance.*

Later, drinking morning 'chai' (tea), I was told that when I prayed in tongues that day I was speaking Russian. Unknown to myself I had apparently glorified God, declaring how awesome and magnificent He is. Someone said, "I thought Ashley has learnt some Russian." It was a miracle, and very reminiscent of the day of Pentecost. This has now happened several times in the Ukraine, but I still can't speak Russian!

Gennadiy edged over to me looking very grave and serious. He hurriedly explained that KGB men had been in the meeting and would be back in fifteen minutes to arrest and deport me. Apparently there was something wrong with my visa. "You have to leave the conference immediately," he insisted.

There was no time to explain, but on the way to our apartment Gennadiy stated that I wouldn't fly out of nearby Dnipropetrovsk, but would have to drive to Kiev. "Why?" I asked, "I have a return plane ticket." He replied, "They will be expecting you at that airport, but the Kiev airport is under another authority and they won't get notification of you for some time."

I rushed into the apartment, grabbed my bags, and jumped back in the car to flee to Kiev, announcing to a few of our pastors and interpreters, "I'll be back." I hoped to keep the promise better than Richard Nixon who had defiantly said the same words, as he walked out of the White House after the Watergate scandal. He never returned. However, I had unfinished business in the city of Pavlograd.

Rob sat in the front while Gennadiy and I bounced amongst the luggage in the back of a tiny white van, as we sped for eight hours to Kiev. If we were caught it would have meant deportation and, worse than that, we would probably have had to cease our work in the Ukraine.

Gennadiy explained that if we were stopped, we should pretend we didn't understand and act dumb. Rob and I laughed and practised looking dumb.

Half way to Kiev at a desperately needed comfort stop, Gennadiy kept a nervous look-out. Finally, late that night we arrived in Kiev with a plan that the following morning we would try to change our plane tickets.

The next morning at the airport, as Rob and I went through ticketing, extra security people arrived and began checking passports, one announcing they were looking for some foreigners. Heart in mouth, we passed through to the transit lounge and were relieved to catch our plane. This was not the end of the story, as six months later we would be back in Pavlograd.

Our friends secured all the necessary permits and the opportunity to hold a public meeting in the largest stadium of Pavlograd. Yes, God had made a way and we were back. Arriving, we found we had been given government permission to have two stadiums at the same time. It was a great joy to look at the beautiful Ukrainian people who we had to suddenly leave only six months before. God was faithful – many miracles occurred during those meetings and, more importantly, people were added to His kingdom.

17 Tonight, I Will Manifest My Glory

In Zhitomir, a city west of Kiev, hundreds of pastors and leaders attended a week of intensive training. In the minibus Rob joined in the Russian conversation. Unable to enter in, I quietly withdrew in my heart, pondering the night's meeting and what God would say to me. "Tonight, I will manifest My glory." A resounding, clear word came from the voice I loved to hear most. The presence of other people in the bus was now irrelevant, as my heart rose with excitement at this word from God.

The vigorous music started and there seemed to be an unusual excitement in the people. As I waited on the Lord to lead the way, I glanced over the people and was greeted by passionate, smiling, singing Ukrainians. I concentrated on working with the Holy Spirit and making space for whatever He wanted to do. If God had a plan for this night and He was going to manifest His glory, obviously I had to decrease and He had to increase.

After I preached a short message to the seven hundred or so people in the theatre, a loud, piercing scream came from a woman seated towards the back of the theatre. A few leaders quickly began to pray for her to be delivered from evil spirits. Not far from the front a second person cried out

145

and other leaders went to pray for her. It seemed as though the presence of Jesus Christ in the meeting was causing demons to come out of people by His sovereign power. The excitement level was rising and I proceeded to give a call for those wanting to give their lives to Christ. "Would you come to Christ tonight?" I urged.

The large, rear door was suddenly flung open and a woman came running down the aisle to the front. I later discovered that this woman had been running around the building, trying to enter the meeting. Each time she tried to enter, an evil spirit would throw her backwards and prevent her from coming inside. At the moment I had asked people to come to Christ, she took a determined run at the door and declared, "I must get into the building now." That woman gave her life to Christ and was saved, delivered and healed that night.

Many people wanted prayer and came forward, hoping for someone to pray for them. As usual, it seemed that there were always more babushkas (grandmothers) than anybody else. Sore knees and backs from doing hard manual labour were the most common ailments.

An elderly woman holding a restless child in her arms made her way to me. As I saw that the child was disabled with spittle dribbling down his chin, my heart sank. 'I am not Jesus,' I thought. I said a short prayer, hoping to comfort the distressed child. Even though the meeting had been successful, the words Jesus spoke to me in the minibus already seemed distant.

Another person led me away towards a man on a stretcher. A blanket covered his body and his face was so thin that the skin seemed to cling to his cheekbones. I was told that four days previously his doctor had said of him, "He has a week left." Now the poor man had just a handful of days left. His wife, crouched beside him, looked tired and distressed. Placing my hands on his forehead, with deep compassion for him I focused my faith on God's love for this man. The service concluded and we left the next day to return to Britain. I continued to thank God for His power and for delivering people. God had given such a clear word on the way to the meeting and had truly manifested His glory that night.

Working with the supernatural God

→ Christianity is supernatural in origin, so as a Christian you need to expect God to do the supernatural today.

→ Keep an active faith in God because He is moved by faith, not just by needs. Trying with a lot of effort to perform a miracle will not force it to happen.

→ You will never be able to plan all the details of a miracle and how it will happen, because it is actually God doing the work.

→ Be conscious that you are working with an invisible person called the Holy Spirit and develop confidence in His presence.

→ Speak and pray out of your love for God and His love for all people.

"... the people who know their God shall be strong, and carry out great exploits."   (Daniel 11:32b)

→ Be at ease, yet full of faith. This will help you to be a good conduit for God's power.

→ Have the attitude that God is always right, and stay humble.

Six months later I was back in the Ukraine in the city of Zhitomir. We were about to close the church service when a man came to me, saying his name was Gregory and I had prayed for him. He seemed very excited about something, gesticulating and tugging at the jacket he was wearing. Through the Russian interpreter I began to put the story together. He was the man on the stretcher six months ago, but now was healed. He explained that the suit he was wearing was now his preaching suit, as he proclaimed to everybody on the streets of Zhitomir that God had healed him. His wife had bought the suit so that he would look nice in his open coffin as he was prepared for burial. Brother Gregory declared with a big smile that this was not his funeral suit but was now his resurrection and preaching suit.

When I was nineteen years old, my father had died of brain cancer and now God had used me to minister His grace to someone in similar need. I was amazed and grateful that now, because God had called me into ministry, someone else's father and grandfather was healed. If we allow Him, God can take the tragedies of life and use them for good.

We were about to leave Zhitomir the next day when I was told that some people wanted to thank me. I was ushered into a room where a boy about six years of age stood with his grandmother and mother. None could speak English so, once again relying on interpreters, the story emerged that this grandmother was the babushka with the handicapped child six months prior. The mother had not been there that night when Jesus had healed their little Rustislav. One short leg had grown and his body had been healed of nine debilitating diseases. Now Rustislav came walking towards me in a little suit and a neat bow tie. This is one of the most awesome feelings that I have ever experienced. We are Christ's ambassadors and carriers of God's amazing grace.

How to pray for the sick

→ Allow yourself to feel the pain of others and think deeply about their suffering. This will develop compassion in your heart.

→ God healed people throughout the Bible. Study the scriptures relating to healing (e.g., Isaiah 53:5, Psalm 103:3 and the life of Jesus). Become utterly convinced that it is God's will to heal the sick.

→ When you are praying, constantly bring your life before God, asking for His healing gift to flow through your life.

→ Dedicate some of your fasts solely for the purpose of God using your life to heal the sick.

→ Be conscious of God's healing power within you and let that awareness override your self consciousness.

→ Have simple faith that you are representing Jesus Christ.

→ Don't allow your mind to dwell on whether this is a difficult, terminal, or life-threatening situation. Be focused and meditate on Jesus' words in Mark 9:23,
"If you can believe, all things are possible to him who believes."

→ Remember, you are a servant of God's power. Be conscious that, when you pray, you are speaking words that are spirit and life.

→ Be aware that some healings are instant while others take place over a period of time.

→ Never tell anyone to cease taking medication. God is well able to heal a person while they are receiving treatment.

→ Thank God for the honour and privilege of being used by Him.

God had certainly been true to the word spoken to me in the minibus on the way to the meeting that night six months before.

I usually take an early evening flight from Kiev to London, and like to sit in a window seat. To keep my heart dreaming of the great commission that is set before me, many times I have pressed my face close to the window to see an almost continuous flow of the large European cities below.

As I looked at all those cities, I recalled that Jesus said,

"Behold, I say to you, lift up your eyes and look at the fields, for they are already white for harvest!"

(John 4:35)

"Go into all the world and preach the gospel to every creature."

(Mark 16:15)

18 *A Dark Day*

I decided to focus on God and consecrate my life further to Him by completing a forty-day fast. I had heard of other people doing this and longed to dedicate more of my life to Jesus, and to discover if His voice would become clearer as I sought Him with all my heart.

Ruth and I had bought an English Tudor style house with an old, disused, World War II bomb shelter buried under the back garden. With a fan for fresh air and carpet on the floor and walls, I converted the bomb shelter into my prayer room. It was my meeting place with God. For forty days Ruth and the other leaders would continue to oversee the church, while I would enjoy spending time in my bomb shelter with God. Soon I was on day twenty-five of my fast. Everything was beautiful and God seemed so close.

That morning our sixteen year old daughter, Melonie, received her GCSE (High School exam) results, and she had achieved very high grades. She had a bad headache and wasn't feeling well, so Ruth had collected her results from the school while Melonie stayed in bed. By the late afternoon her eyes could take no light, so Ruth drew the curtains. By evening, Melonie's condition worsened and she began to appear somewhat delirious. During the day she had mentioned a purplish-red mark that had appeared on her arm, but we had no reason to be concerned about it. Ruth contacted a doctor who said Melonie must be dehydrated and to keep her drinking water, but by evening we were trying in vain to spoon water into her mouth. She began to have convulsions, so David Harland of our Brighton church came around to pray for her. We tried to remain calm as we wondered what to do next and how much worse this illness would become.

Could it be just be a passing virus? We had never seen Melonie like this before and the situation was definitely becoming worse. Realising that this was now extremely serious with her health rapidly deteriorating by the hour, Ruth insisted that a doctor come to our house. The doctor agreed to come. In the early hours of the morning we quietly led the doctor to Melonie's room, describing the convulsions and our attempts to spoon water into her mouth. After a few moments the doctor lifted the blanket to examine her further. Noticing marks on her legs and arms, he immediately asked where our telephone was. Without discussion, he requested an ambulance urgently be brought to our house and within minutes one was waiting outside. The doctor had immediately realised the seriousness of Melonie's condition and knew that every minute was now critical to saving her life.

Apart from the occasional spasm, our beautiful daughter was now totally unconscious, so was strapped to a chair to be taken down the stairs and to the waiting ambulance. In the back she was once again strapped down, this time to a horizontal bed, while I sat on a seat alongside her. In the back of the ambulance my mind was in a whirl. As Ruth followed by car, I heard the siren occasionally sounding while we charged through red lights on the way to the hospital. I looked at Melonie, now lying unconscious. How could things change so quickly? A few hours beforehand I had been praying in my bomb shelter, and as a family we had been very pleased with her excellent exam results.

The ambulance pulled up outside the hospital and reversed into the Accident and Emergency area. As the doors opened, the medical staff waited with a stretcher. The doctors had been notified and were now ready to work on her, as she was transferred onto the stretcher and wheeled through the corridors. Everything around us seemed to blur. Accident and Emergency is not a pretty sight at 2:00am. Melonie was taken into a small room and five doctors began to examine her. Still unconscious, apart from an occasional convulsion, her body lay still. A brain scan was quickly arranged and showed massive infection.

A doctor signalled to Ruth and me to leave her room so he could talk to us in private. He pulled down his white face mask and began slowly, "We will do our best to save your daughter, but her condition is very serious and appears to be bacterial meningitis. Tests will take several days to confirm but we don't have that time to spare, so every antibiotic for meningitis is going into her system now." He did not tell us until the next day that the doctors did not expect Melonie to survive the night and that, if she did, there would most likely be permanent brain damage.

Ruth and I went to her bedside again. Holding hands, we had many thoughts and questions but few answers. To be honest, I felt absolutely hopeless. Would I preach again? Could I preach on healing and miracles? I knew this sickness was not from God, but why? And where was God?

I felt my heart align itself to a position of faith in God and my mind began to focus on the reality of the situation that was before us. On the outside nothing had changed, but in my heart something had shifted. "God," I cried, "even if Melonie dies tonight and her funeral is within days, I will never stop believing that You are a good God and You still heal today." The force of these thoughts surprised me and

I decided that, if Melonie should live, the demons of hell would not get off lightly. They never should have attacked us in the first place. I said in my heart, "Devil, you will regret the day that you messed with my family. Whether Melonie lives or dies tonight, you are going to regret it!"

This was the longest night of our lives, looking at our unconscious daughter with her beautiful, curly, red hair lying loose on the clean, white sheets of the Brighton hospital bed. Doctors regularly peered into her eyes and sometimes pricked her fingers with a needle, hoping for a reaction to pain. There was no reaction. Without any anaesthetic, a needle for drawing out fluid was put directly into her spine.

What was happening? Where was God? How could things change so quickly? The euphoria of her exam results, the peace and tranquillity of our home and the prayerful seclusion of my bomb shelter were now all gone, all within a few hours.

Early the next morning I returned to our home to telephone some of our Australian pastors who were gathered at a conference. They agreed to pray and spread the word for urgent prayer on behalf of Melonie. Over the following hours members of our Brighton church also prayed fervently for God's mercy and healing.

Going through painful experiences

→ Keep your focus on your life's purpose.

→ Identify people of strength who are close to you.

→ Ask others to pray with and for you.

→ Love God.

→ Believe God's Word.

> "And we know that all things work together for good to those who love God, to those who are the called according to His purpose."   (Romans 8:28)

→ *Stay thankful, no matter whatever happens.*

→ *Think logically about all your options.*

→ *Don't make major decisions while you are feeling low emotionally.*

→ *Realise that the pain won't last forever.*

I returned to be alongside my daughter in the hospital ward. It had been the longest night of our lives and we were exhausted. At about 10:00am, the doctors and nurses had temporarily left the room and all was quiet. Suddenly Melonie spoke, "Shut up, Amy!" Her younger sister, Amy, was nowhere near the hospital ward and Melonie was dreaming. For once I was glad to hear her tell Amy to shut up!

The fever had broken, consciousness had returned, and she slowly began to speak. She had been to the edge of life and had come back. Melonie spent about two weeks in hospital recovering. We are grateful to the medical staff who did all they could do to save our daughter. They did not expect her to survive but the prayers of many people were answered and God had spared her life.

For me, it was back to the bomb shelter to complete the forty days of prayer and fasting. With a very joyful heart I knew that our enemy had attacked, but the prayers of the saints had prevailed.

19 *Running With The Vision*

"If he can do that, so can I," I stated confidently to Ruth while sprawled on the sofa, watching on TV a ninety-three year old Sikh man run the London Marathon. "Well, do it!" Ruth replied. It was easy enough to decide from the lounge chair, but running 26.2 miles (42 km) involved more than just a decision. From April 2004 to March 2005 I spent almost every spare moment training for the big run.

I ran and ran, at my gym, through Brighton city centre and along the sea front. Reminded of the 'Forrest Gump' film, sometimes I talked to myself, "Run, Forrest, run. Run, Ashley, run!" When it comes to calculating mileage in a pair of running shoes instead of car tyres, you know that running has become a serious business.

On the big day there was a festive feeling in the air. The athletes gathered and a helicopter hovered overhead, taking pictures of the runners stretching and warming up. We were about to run a course through the streets of London, and my only plan was to complete the race. I said confidently to the stranger next to me, "See you at the finish." The gun fired, and 35,000 runners surged forward. The sheer numbers headed in one direction – galloping, dashing, sprinting. It was as though we were being madly chased by a dinosaur from Jurassic Park.

The runners began to spread out as some moved faster along the course. We ran over London Bridge, alongside the River Thames and past Big Ben, but as energy levels ebbed no one was thinking about these historic landmarks. By the 20 mile mark, huffing and puffing I asked myself, "Why did you tell everyone you were going to do this? Now you have to finish it." The crowds were encouraging and bands played cheerfully along the route, but even to raise a smile took energy and I grimaced instead. One woman in the crowd saw the look on my face and shouted, "Sir, there are only 6 miles left!" It was meant as encouragement. Exhausted, I reprimanded myself, "Why didn't you just stick to preaching?"

Runners on the side of the road rubbed their calf muscles and stretched to relieve cramps. I passed an ambulance giving oxygen to a collapsed runner. It seemed like there were more runners sitting or lying on the road than running. At the 25 mile mark there were only 1.2 miles left. 'I have to run... I think I can... I know I can.' These thoughts fed through my mind like ticker tape. Officials had encouraged all runners to lift up their arms as they crossed the finish line. Past Buckingham Palace and there was only 0.2 mile on the last stretch. Speeding up, I gave it all I had and raised my arms for the photograph. Someone put a medal around my neck, and seconds later I vomited. But who cares? It was now over and the race had been completed. They say there are only two groups of people in life – those who have run marathons and those who haven't!

The late, great church leader, Brother Lester Sumrall, came to preach in our Innisfail church many years ago and I took a moment to ask him something that I had always wanted to ask a seasoned preacher. "How do you stay in ministry a long time?" Brother Sumrall responded tersely,

"Think pumpkins, not peanuts – and just remember, it's not how you start the race but how you finish."

Although many people joined us and were trained in leadership, we were blessed to have mature Christian leaders and pastors join our team, resulting in the founding of strong churches in towns and cities across the United Kingdom. For many years Julian Melfi had been a passionate Christian leader in the London area. He and his wife, Sharon, established Christian Outreach Centre's thriving Citygate Church which has had strategic community and local government influence in the London Borough of Bromley. The skills of Julian and other great leaders helped broaden the impact of the growing Christian Outreach Centre movement in the UK.

Our Brighton church's first building was a leased warehouse that served us well, but we always knew that one day a permanent church home and offices would have to be purchased. Owning a building always provides stability, reduces financial restraints and enables the vision to move forward. From the time of acquiring our leased premises, we eagerly sought the building that we would truly call our church 'home'.

As in every organisation, leadership enables a church to either rise or fall. To buy a building in Brighton I knew was going to be both a test of leadership and faith in God.

A suitable building was eventually found, but that was the easy part. Making it ours and bringing the vision into reality required many fund raising strategies. The church did not have much surplus money, but I decided to distribute a ten pound note to every member of the church. We asked people to invest their ten pounds in a project of their choice and to bring back the increased amount on a certain day in a few months' time. People developed many creative ideas, such as buying cooking ingredients and selling biscuits, giving guitar lessons and emptying the contents of their attics to sell at car boot sales.

That Sunday, some visitors attending church for the first time were surprised and startled to be given ten pounds. It was exciting to see the momentum created by the investment and how it increased. From children to old age pensioners, people brought their increase and gave into the vision.

As everyone in the church worked together to raise funds, it brought to mind the early church selling their possessions and laying the proceeds at the feet of the apostles.

We planned to renovate the new premises and, while in prayer one morning, God spoke to me from 2 Chronicles chapter 2: *Then Solomon determined to build a temple for the name of the Lord...* (and Hiram king of Tyre responded) *"I have sent a skilful man endowed with understanding, Huram, my master craftsman."* A few days later, Dave, my Australian friend who had previously organised the building of our Solomon Islands ministry training facilities called me, "Don't worry. I will do it for you." He was to be our 'master craftsman'!

The large building was quickly renovated and became the base for our operations in Europe. It is an honour to have friends who stand together and a God who speaks to us when we don't quite know how, when, where or what to do.

How to recognise potential leaders

→ They push existing boundaries.

→ They often have big ideas and are bored by the status quo. Some people may think they are proud.

→ Potential leaders will ask a lot of questions, but will only learn from people they admire and have decided to follow.

→ They will often have strong feelings on certain issues and principles.

→ There is a general intensity about their lives towards achieving something. Time is valuable to these people.

→ Potential leaders are consistent and active as functional church members. They pray and read the Bible a lot.

→ Their peers listen when they speak.

→ People who live life with them are changed and affected by their relationship.

→ Understand that there are various styles of leadership. Don't just expect one style.

Shepherds at heart, our church pastors David and Jackie Harland grew quickly in leadership. Their love for Brighton and partnering in the church vision was crucial to the advancement of the work. The Brighton church, now known as CityCoast Church, was in good hands. They led this amazing church while Ruth and I focused on the United Kingdom and the rapidly expanding work across Europe.

We ran with the vision that God showed me before leaving Australia of the red dots on the map of Europe which was now steadily progressing. I realised that there is no limit to the nations that we can reach with the gospel. It is just a matter of training more church leaders and staying focused on the words of Jesus Christ.

20 *Will You Be My Father?*

French was not my favourite subject at high school and I managed to hover near bottom of the class for most exams. Why learn French when I was planning to live in an Australian country town for the rest of my life? One night our teachers tried to impress upon us students the culture of France by hosting a French evening. Amongst a variety of French food, frog legs were on the menu. I always wondered what happened to the rest of the frog.

For two years I attended French classes until finally persuading my teachers that I could study geography by correspondence in a separate classroom, thereby replacing this seemingly unnecessary subject. As I sat alone in a classroom doing my geography correspondence lessons, I was thrilled to have beaten 'the system', leaving French behind forever.

Thirty years later at a school reunion I found that none of my former classmates had ever visited France. And I?

"Bonjour! Merci," people greeted as I walked into the church in Dunkerque, northern France. A distant memory twitched in the recesses of my brain, as I recognised words from my French class decades before. I searched to see if anything else was there, but unfortunately there was little to recall! 'Ferme la bouche' – I was sure the teacher had said something about that from time to time.

161

Making my way to the front of the church, suddenly a bearded French man lunged forward and rubbed his hairy face on my cheek then the other side of my face. I blushed deeply at his unexpected kiss. No one had told me about this in French class. My face began to itch and I felt my rural Australian culture challenged. I also realised why Ruth had always insisted on a clean shave.

Jean Biville was the pastor of the Dunkerque church I visited that weekend, and the year after our first meeting this great man died of a heart attack. The father of the Dunkerque church was gone and it was important for his people to find security. The leadership of this church looked to us for guidance and strength for the way forward. I had lost a friend and partner in the gospel but others had lost their husband, father and pastor. It reminded me so much of the loss of my own father. I saw in the faces of Jean's widow, Marie, his family and church members the same vulnerability I had seen in my mother and her younger children. I knew my job was to care for the Dunkerque church and now be their father, just as I had been many years before with my younger siblings. Jean's daughter, Lydie, and her husband, Michel, became the new pastors.

My Grandad who had inspired me in my early years had been injured fighting in France in World War I. He was shot in the shoulder outside the city of Amiens, less than an hour's drive from our growing churches in northern France. Samuel Dales was involved in a muddy and violent battle for France but now we had a new army advancing and growing in strength across the land.

I recall a telephone conversation in 1994 with my good friend, Rob Smillie. He and his wife, Julie, had come to establish a church in Scotland before Ruth and I arrived in the United Kingdom. At that time Rob was feeling very isolated and was going through an incredibly difficult time in the ministry. "Ashley, I know you now have many sons. I have seen the way that you are raising them up. My question is, 'Can you adopt one?' I desperately need a father." I instantly felt the pain and longing of Rob's heart. He was reaching out for help. I paused and then responded, "Rob, many years ago Ruth and I had to adopt many sons and daughters when we took over the Innisfail church and the founding pastor moved on. We had to adopt many people at that time. So the answer is 'Yes!'" I could feel the sigh of relief over the phone and slowly the conversation became much lighter.

Rob realised what he needed and pursued it in order to become a true son who then would become a spiritual father to many in Europe. I have found this to be a similar situation with many people.

Called by God from a young age, Bojidar worked as an interpreter and preacher during the great revival that swept Bulgaria in the early years after the breakup of the Soviet Union. At the centre of the Balkan nations, Bulgaria is now a member state of the European Union. Bojidar's grandfather had been publicly executed before his son's eyes during the ruthless reign of the communists. Bojidar desired to make a difference in his land through the love of Christ and by training church leaders to bring permanent change in the Balkans. For many years now I have worked with Bojidar, helping him train leaders for Bulgaria and the surrounding nations. From Plovdiv, the second largest city in Bulgaria, he leads the battle to retake the Balkans for Christ.

Cairo is officially rated as 'the noisiest city on earth.' The constant beeping of horns, calls to prayer from numerous mosques and the jackhammers of countless building sites all add to the decibels of this huge city of over twenty million inhabitants.

Our driver sped from Cairo airport towards the city. Very soon we approached a red light but the car kept its momentum, moving forward and through the intersection. I tensed and pointed out that the light had been clearly red. The driver laughed and said, "Here in Egypt traffic lights are like Christmas trees – they flash but we don't notice them." Everything is covered in dust and I have been jokingly told by my Egyptian friends that the dust provides them with vitamins.

Christians in Egypt are proud that Jesus visited this ancient land as a child. Filled with history and landmarks, pharonic pyramids and biblical bulrushes add flavour to this amazing place. Amongst the hustling car traffic may be a donkey and cart, a camel or bicycle – all moving with no rules apart from 'get ahead by any means possible.' I have often wondered how pedestrians survived.

Having never expected that God would put this nation in my heart, I visited it a few times. I had come to visit the Pyramids, do a little preaching, have a brief holiday in Egypt and meet again with Fakhry and Mary Hanna who I had met several years before.

Fakhry pulled his old car over to the side of the dusty street in Cairo. The car's muffler was partially falling off and the noise it made blended musically into Cairo's background orchestra. My new friend turned to look at me and asked seriously, "Please, will you be my spiritual father? I need a father." "If I am your father, I might sometimes have to discipline you," I replied. Fakhry laughed and insisted, "That is okay, but please be my spiritual father." "Let's walk together and see what God does," I explained. I was impressed by Fakhry's deliberate and specific request. He had thought much about it, had wondered how to ask me and where to park the car – all because he knew what he wanted and needed for his ministry. I must confess that when Fakhry asked me that question, my immediate thought was, 'I might have to visit this noisy, dusty place more often.' This divine connection with Fakhry has resulted in many Arabic leaders being trained and churches being planted across several nations of the Middle East.

Working with leaders

→ *Don't bore them.*

→ *Give them guidelines, but not too much restriction that will inhibit their creativity to do the job.*

→ *Require accountability which raises people to a higher level of leadership because they know what they do is valued.*

→ *Notice little things they have done and acknowledge these, not just the big things.*

→ *Give personal words of encouragement, showing them that you care.*

→ *Match the job with the person's present strength of character and their present level of leadership gift.*

→ *Don't speak negatively about them or undermine the responsibility that has been entrusted to them.*

→ *Let them do things differently to how you would do it.*

→ *Don't embarrass them in front of their peers or followers.*

→ *Don't create an over familiar environment where it is easy for them to cross the boundary of respect.*

→ *Trust is the most precious quality in any relationship, so honour their trust in you.*

→ *Strength of character carries the leadership gift. Take time to ask the probing questions concerning character and walk with them as they apply the various principles to strengthen the weak areas.*

→ *Although this can't always be done, it is best to give a positional title after you have observed them doing the task. This is a sure indication that they will continue to do it, because a title won't keep them motivated.*

On one visit to Egypt Ruth, our daughters and I ventured on a camel ride. Amongst the twenty or so other travellers my camel was last in the long line. Last is not the place I like to be in life. Our guide had given each of us a baton to prod the camel's rump if it stopped moving. I proceeded to tap my camel to encourage it to move faster up the line. Progress was slow but, after a few good whacks, it began to gallop. We soon passed the long line of other travellers and my camel was still galloping at a good pace. As my chequered scarf waved in the breeze, I felt like Lawrence of Arabia. With every bounce I realised there is no suspension on a camel, and my poor backside felt every gallop. On reaching our destination I dismounted, feeling proud of my camel racing. Upon closer inspection, I found that the skin on my tail bone had worn off.

Next day flying back to England, I tried miserably to find a way to sit without touching my poor, skinless tail bone.

Indian trains rival any other travel experience. Rattling along one night at 2am, as Indian waiters delivered tea and coffee to weary travellers who could not sleep, I talked with my fellow traveller, an Indian church leader.

He and I discussed the amazing work of the Holy Spirit – how He changes people's lives and the difference He makes in churches. The conversation became more passionate between the two of us and we began to forget about where we were, the time of night or the weariness of our bodies. Suddenly the Indian church leader shouted at me, "He is in the train here now!" His eyes and facial expression said it all. He knew the Holy Spirit and he recognised His presence. I decided it was no surprise that God was using that man.

Several years prior to my first trip to India, the Australian missionary, Graham Staines, and two of his sons were burnt to death in India by Hindu extremists. These incredible missionaries were relatives of mine who literally gave their lives in their love for India.

Nepal, nestled amongst the majestic Himalayas, is a nation almost encompassed by its giant neighbours of India and China. This strategic nation is home to the famous Ghurkhas whose bravery is legendary in the British army. The Ghurkha regiments have received by far the greatest number of prestigious medals in the British military.

Sitting in a cafe in Brisbane, I met my first Nepalese man. Raju presented me with a Nepalese hat and a photo of him with his family. I wondered whatever I was supposed to do with this strange, little cap which was certainly not much use in providing shade from the sun. I took it back to England and every now and then would pull out this cap, look at it and then tuck it away in my desk drawer. Sometimes I looked at the photo that Raju gave me and wondered when we would meet again.

Nepal is also a nation hungry for the reality of God, where Christians were first recorded in the 1950's. A Hindu nation for 237 years, in 2007 Nepal became a secular nation, meaning Christianity and other religions could be freely practised.

Our vision for Nepal began slowly, and a heart for Nepalese people grew in me when I first visited the country in October 2005.

In October 2007 Ruth and I were granted the privilege to meet the Prime Minster of Nepal at his personal residence. I remembered the words of TL Osborn, "When you are in the presence of the head of any nation or a political leader, you must carry yourself as a statesman."

Early that morning we waited in the Prime Minister's official room where he met various visiting dignitaries. My friend, Raju, had arranged this meeting and there was a suppressed and reserved excitement amongst us as we sat, aware of the privilege. The doors opened before us and in came the Prime Minster of Nepal. He was smartly dressed in his official Nepalese garments and cap, carrying himself with authority. We stood to greet him and he came towards us with a warm, welcoming smile.

Signalling for our group to sit on his official chairs, he turned to me and asked, "Why do you want to see me?" "I want to thank you for making your country a place where Christianity can be taught," I responded. This Hindu Prime Minster who had spent many years in prison on his quest for democracy replied, "I quote Jesus often. Jesus said, 'Love your neighbour,' and that is what I endeavour to do."

How great is our God, that even a Hindu head of state would proclaim and endeavour to live by the words of Jesus Christ? After some moments of conversation I asked if he would allow me to pray for him. This he did and bowed his head as I asked God to give him wisdom and guidance to lead his nation. I blessed Nepal's Prime Minister for his courage to lead by his strong convictions and thanked him for his time. While we departed, his government colleagues were arriving for their cabinet session.

Going from average to great leadership

→ Understand that being in leadership is a lifestyle, not a destination.

→ Identify and isolate insecurity in your life, so that it does not define your relationships and, thereby, your leadership.

→ Master the skill of working with stronger leaders.

→ Don't stop paying the price.

→ Have an attitude that no one owes you anything. Keep living for others.

→ Choose your close friends, knowing that some who were once your close friends may slowly become only acquaintances.

→ Keep living by your established values.

→ Take personal time to dream and stay fresh.

→ Value your time because it is your greatest asset.

→ Keep gaining input from others more influential than you.

→ Maintain honour in your heart towards authority.

→ Beware of developing a critical or cynical spirit.

→ Stay humble, no matter how much success comes your way.

→ In times of difficulty great leaders know how to rule over their emotions and diligently seek God for the answers.

Now David was greatly distressed, for the people spoke of stoning him, because the soul of all the people was grieved, every man for his sons and daughters. But David strengthened himself in the Lord his God.

(1 Samuel 30:6)

Conclusion

In January 2009 I was elected as International President of Christian Outreach Centre. This is the same group of churches that in 1975 I had forbidden my girlfriend to attend, saying, "Ruth, if you are going to be my wife, I don't want you going back to that place."

It is an honour to have been asked to lead this great movement of churches. I have learned to never underestimate what God can do in and through one person's life.

It was not long ago that I first heard God speak to me on the night of the hail storm in October 1983. "Ashley, you have always believed in Me. Why haven't you taken Me seriously? My relationship with you is the most important thing in your life. You have always wanted fruit. If you follow Me, you will have fruit for eternity!"

I have discovered that life is very short and yet we each have an amazing opportunity to affect the lives of many people.

In our travels Ruth and I had not yet visited Chile, but Fred and Mary had. This was the same Fred with me in the Solomon Islands who had responded so wisely when asked by a Papua New Guinea student, "What do I do with a man who comes to my church and he has three wives with children by each wife?" Fred had responded with compassion and the heart of a true shepherd.

170

In March 2009 Ruth and I finally had the privilege of visiting Chile. Dozens of Chilean churches were founded, established and continue to grow because Fred and Mary, a plumber and a former nun, learned Spanish and left Australia to live in this country and train many people. Ruth and I had impacted the lives of Fred and Mary who, in turn, had affected and changed the lives of large numbers of people in a country I had previously not visited.

I find it amazing to reproduce your life into someone else who then goes on to multiply disciples. This is how real Christianity has spread through the centuries. Seeing this work in Chile was one of the greatest moments of my life.

On the 20th of August 2009 I sat beside my grandmother, Miriam Schmierer, the oldest person in Australia, as she celebrated her 110th birthday. Australia's media waited and microphones were thrust across the table at my frail but quick thinking Grandma, as she sat confidently peering into the faces of reporters. "Mrs Schmierer, you have lived through two world wars and the Great Depression and have seen a lot in your long life. Tell us what you think of life today."

Grandma thought for a brief moment and responded, "It's worse today." The room went quiet. The surprised reporter queried, "What do you mean?" Was she commenting on the present recession and comparing it with the Great Depression?

"In the wars and the Great Depression people talked to each other and had time for each other, but today people are so busy they don't talk enough to each other. We have become too busy."

Hamsters are quite a common pet in Britain and, when our girls were young, they easily persuaded us to buy one. For countless hours each day, with sweat on its little face,

Hammie the Hamster ran on his little wheel. At nights we had to disable the wheel to prevent it from rattling away during the night. One day the wheel stopped turning and the hamster fell out, dead. Our pet's life was cut short by a heart attack as he tried unsuccessfully to outrun his wheel. Life is just like that for so many, running faster and faster but never quite able to get in front. We can all learn from the hamster and take a step sideways into a happier and slower life, where we have time for each other and not just for ourselves.

I am often reminded of the story in Luke chapter 10 regarding the Good Samaritan, and the question asked in verse 29, "Who is my neighbour?" Jesus tells the parable and then instructs in verse 37, "Go and do likewise." The two men who first passed by had their reasons for not stopping. Maybe they were too busy or afraid, but then one came along who stopped and changed the life of the injured man forever. We should make time for each other and allow compassion to govern our hearts. Remember that everybody has value, and the potential within each person is staggering.

I have seen many cities and nations, once in spiritual darkness, open up to the revival power of God's Spirit. From Australia and the Pacific island nations to Europe and the other continents of the world, I have witnessed what God can do in people's lives, if they walk with Him.

I have seen many sons and daughters become true fathers and mothers, and the fatherless learn the ways of a father's heart and become effective fathers themselves.

I have seen that God has put something of His nature into every culture. When people of many nations work together, we learn much from each other.

I have seen the faithfulness of God to fulfil His Word wherever and whenever people believe Him. They may be people who have few earthly possessions or low social status, but God loves all people.

I have seen amazing miracles – the blind person seeing, the cripple walking, and freedom for the demon-possessed.

I have seen that, although the job may appear colossal, together we can do it, because people matter to God!

I have seen God transform my life from a shy individual who could not speak to people into one who influences national leaders and nations.

Jesus prayed to His heavenly Father concerning His own life:

"I have glorified You on the earth. I have finished the work which You have given Me to do."

(John 17:4)

As Jesus did, we give glory to God for all that we accomplish in our lives. You and I have not yet finished our work, so let us be about our heavenly Father's business of reaching our world for Christ.

As you rise, you can take others with you and see fruit that lasts for eternity.

Contact Ashley Schmierer at:
Christian Outreach Centre World Office
North Street, Portslade, BN41 1DG
Brighton & Hove
East Sussex, United Kingdom
Tel: +44 (0)1273 433433
Fax: +44 (0)1273 433423
www.cocworld.com
or email us on admin@cocworld.com

We hope you enjoyed reading this
New Wine book.
For details of other New Wine books
and a wide range of titles from other
Word and Spirit publishers visit our website:
www.newwineministries.co.uk
or email us on newwine@xalt.co.uk